The Complete IQ Test Book

"The more we apply mental power against seemingly hopeless difficulties and follow the flashes of insight which come from real thinking, the surer our accomplishment. Thinking gives one the daring to do the unusual when a situation calls for it: a readiness to shift thinking quickly when problems turn out differently than anticipated.

Dr Norman Vincent Peale

The Complete IQ Test Book

John Bremner

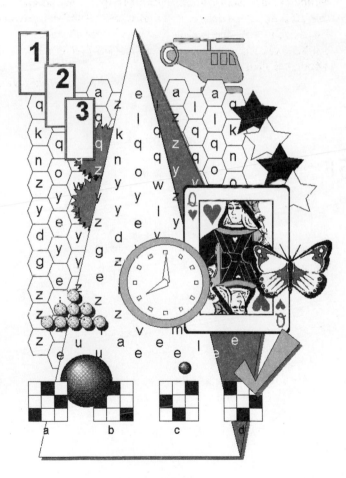

EBURY PRESS

1 3 5 7 9 10 8 6 4 2

First published in 1997 by
Ebury Press
Random House UK Ltd
Random House
20 Vauxhall Bridge Road
London SW1V 2SA

Random House Australia (Pty) Ltd
20 Alfred Street
Milsons Point Sydney
New South Wales 2016 Australia

Random House New Zealand Limited
18 Poland Road, Glanfield
Aukland 10 New Zealand

Random House South Africa (Pty) Ltd
PO Box 337 Bergvlei South Africa
Random House UK Limited Reg. No. 954009

A CIP catalogue record for this book is available from the British Library.

ISBN 0 09 185332 X

Typeset from Author's disks by Clive Dorman & Co.
Printed and bound in Great Britain by Butler & Tanner, Frome.

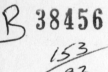

Contents

•••

Acknowledgements

●●●

I would like to thank my family and friends and all the volunteers who allowed themselves to be tested during the preparation of this book. In particular, thanks to my son Richard for being the first guinea pig for most of the tests, and for his many suggestions for improvements, and to David Ballheimer for his meticulous editing.

Introduction

•••••••••••••••••••••••••••••••••••••

Our IQ (intelligence quotient) is essentially a measure of our own intelligence against that of the rest of society, but it can also be a measure of our self-esteem. Many people have been pleasantly surprised to discover, after doing an IQ test, that they were more intelligent than they had thought. With this updated measure of their abilities they can gain a new confidence in life. If you discover that your IQ puts you in the top – say, 20 per cent, when you had thought you were merely average, you are likely to reassess your life and to adjust your personal goals. The knowledge that you are more intelligent than 80 per cent of those around you can give you the incentive to go for promotion, or to quit your job and start on your own. Perhaps you will go for that degree that until now you never thought you were capable of? Perhaps you will just hold your head higher and value your own judgement more. Whatever the case, you are unlikely to remain the same.

Fortunately it is unlikely that any reader of this book will discover their intelligence to be below average. Many people who will buy this book already suspect that they are not using their full potential. Only those of above average intelligence tend to show any curiosity as to their intellectual abilities. Perhaps you have picked up clues to your intelligence – do you have an understanding of abstract concepts that baffle others? Have you always felt different, and had trouble fitting in? Are you more sensitive, or more aware than your peers? Perhaps you are not satisfied to believe what others tell you?

Paradoxically, the more intelligent you are, the greater will be the tendency to underestimate your ability. The greatest personal value of IQ tests therefore, is to correct this problem and give us a real idea of our own ability. Only when we know ourselves can we go on to fulfil our true potential.

The tests

The tests in this book are designed to measure the five main aspects of intelligence – the ability to recognise and decode visual patterns – *visual-spatial* cognitive ability; the ability to recognise numerical patterns and solve problems, *numerical* ability; the ability to use our native language, *verbal-linguistic* ability; the ability to come to true conclusions about stated facts, *logical deduction*; and the ability to put all these other skills to practical use, *creative* ability. Each test is complete in itself, and may be used to determine a score for a specific subject, but all the tests need to be taken into account to determine your overall IQ. The procedure for this is on page 109, together with a graph on page 110 that converts your test results into an IQ score.

If the procedures for completing the tests in this book are followed carefully, they will give a fair estimate of your IQ, within the limits imposed by non-standard test conditions, and the space restrictions of this book. However, no IQ test can claim to be definitive, and you are likely to find that each test you take evaluates your IQ in a slightly different way, producing a different overall score.

Do not examine any of the test problems before commencing the tests, even if you do not intend to start the test immediately – once we look at a problem our subconscious mind begins working on it, and makes the solution come easier. In the same way, if you sit the tests and then come back to them later and redo them, you will find an increase in your score simply because you remember how to do some of them. Mensa have found it necessary to wait three years before re-testing, to eliminate the memory factor.

If, on the other hand, your intention is to boost your IQ score, then do the tests as often as you like. The very act of completing IQ tests actually increases our IQ score. Part of this increased score is due to test-sophistication – becoming familiar with typical problems and their methods of solution, but part of the increase is because of a genuine boost in our intelligence level. We do our thinking with physical connections in our brain – axons and dendrites, and the more we practise at any task, the greater the number of neural connections for that task.

It is a common fallacy that our brain remains unchanged once we reach adulthood. We can't grow more neurones – the grey cells, but the connections between those cells are in a state of continual flux, constantly throwing out or breaking connections in an unbelievably complex communications network, with up to 10,000 connections between each cell.

When we persist at any task for sufficiently long, the connections become permanent, and the axons grow a myelin sheathing, analogous to the shielding in a coaxial cable, that protects them and helps them to function efficiently. Laboratory tests have shown that the more neural connections we gain, the more intelligent we become.[1]

The neural network is unbelievably complex.

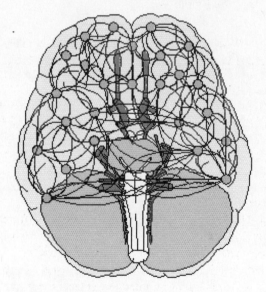

---

[1] For more information on this subject, see *How to Boost Your IQ*, by John Bremner (Ward-Lock/Cassell)

IQ distribution

Around 50 per cent of the population fall within the *normal* range of between 90 and 110. Very few people within this range achieve academic distinction, although much depends on the character of the individual, and the subjects being studied. Determination and hard study can be a good substitute for intelligence. It can even foster that quality. Occasionally, exceptional people towards the top of the *normal* range manage to become officers in the armed forces.

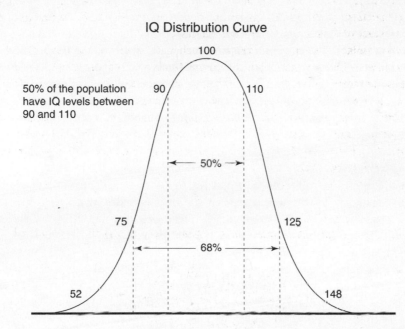

IQ Distribution Curve

Most people who stay on at school taking academic subjects beyond the minimum leaving age are at the bright end of normal. Teachers come into the top six per cent with average IQs of around 130. Only around four per cent of the population have IQs of 140, and around 70 per cent of those at this level and above, according to a Californian study, are in professional or managerial positions – college lecturers, doctors, top business people, writers, and professors.

The IQ/job performance relationship

Studies have shown that IQ tests are a better predictor of future performance in both education and work, than any other form of selection, providing a more accurate indication of who is likely to succeed than even the most experienced personnel director or teacher.[2]

In fact, interview based selection has negative predictive power, which is to say that those persons we instinctively feel will be good based on interview selection, are those people who do the least well, with lower production, more on-the-job mistakes, more time off sick, and poorer results in job evaluation tests. Interview based selection tests only the skill of the applicant at being interviewed, which is not the skill required in most jobs.

---

[2] As an employer I tested this in practise and found that IQ based pre-testing plus interview is far more effective at choosing candidates who will do well than qualification and interview based selection. Present abilities are not always related to past performance. J.B.

IQ tests, on the other hand, measure the ability to perform a large number of mental tasks effectively, and these are the same abilities that effective employees have – in jobs that require intelligence as the prime asset.

In jobs that require skill as the prime asset, the most effective method of selection is a skill-test. I once dealt with a company that selected carpenters by interview – they got good talkers, but they did not get good carpenters.

Mensa

To qualify for entrance to Mensa, you must score, in a supervised IQ test, within the top two per cent of the population. A score of 148 and above on the Cattell scale, which should be roughly comparable to the scoring scale in this book, gets you into Mensa. If you score around 130 on the tests within this book, it could be worth having a try for membership, given that scores can vary from day-to-day, and that this book cannot measure your IQ as accurately as a supervised test under controlled conditions.

There are Mensa testing centres in many major cities throughout the world. The main addresses can be found on page 126.

Scores

Once you have determined your IQ score, you may like to examine the table of occupations overleaf and see if your occupation is within the expected set for your score. If it is in a higher set than expected, great. You have succeeded in overcoming difficulties and achieved beyond expectations. If your occupation falls into a lower than expected bracket, perhaps you should consider aiming for something more challenging to your intellectual abilities.

It is worth noting that the table only provides tendencies. There are exceptions to the career/IQ relationships illustrated here. Some highly intelligent people are happy doing manual labour. Tony Buzan, author of *Use Your Head*, and originator of Mind-Mapping spent a year shovelling dung, and he recalls it as one of the happiest times of his life.

Discovering that your IQ is higher than you expected can transform your life. Victor Serebriakoff, founder and honorary international president of Mensa, tells of how the discovery that he had a high IQ, after taking an army IQ test, changed all his expectations and led to a life of achievement that he would never have thought possible.

Some people of high intelligence are trapped by circumstances into jobs that are far beneath them. Others may be simply lazy, and can't be bothered obtaining the qualifications that would enable them to move up. That is a pity, because it has been shown that every extra year in education is worth around sixteen per cent extra income. We tend to get into our occupations before we gain an appreciation of our own potential. Then, once we qualify in that area we are unlikely to change careers unless external events force us to do so.

There are many secretaries, carpenters, labourers, and salespersons with IQ levels above most doctors, but their potential remains dormant.

The following table is far from comprehensive. If you do not find your occupation here, use the nearest equivalents. The physical position of each occupation within the table is also meant to show where that occupation lies according to IQ – the higher the position, the higher the IQ. But of course, nothing is written in stone. Studies of applicants for membership of Mensa have shown that there is a spread of occupations throughout IQ levels. That said, it is rare to find an academic with an IQ of less than 130, or a road-sweeper with an IQ of over 120.

Please do not be offended if your occupation appears to be in a lower category here than you would expect. This table is intended as a rough guide only, and is based on average IQ levels. As you will be aware, to obtain an average we must take into account scores which are very much above the average, as well as those which are below the average.

IQ Score	Table of typical occupations against IQ levels
150	professors, lecturers, top surgeons & specialists, managing directors, physicists, musicians,
140	mathematicians, authors, academics, chemists
130	doctors, teachers, politicians, engineers, computer programmers, electricians, nurses,
120	architects, self-employed, sales, police
110	trades-persons, shopkeepers, factory workers,
100	farmers, local councillors, drivers
90	semi-skilled, cleaners, garbage collectors, farm
80	labourers, miners, road-sweepers

Children

The tests in this book are designed for people aged 16+, of at least average intelligence. If you are younger than that age and you wish to take the tests, you should be aware that the tests will underestimate your intelligence. You can compensate for this to some extent by dividing your IQ score (according to the graph on page 110) by your age to the nearest whole year, multiplying that result by 16, and adding 5 for every year that you are younger than 16.

Development

Some psychologists claim that our IQ reaches an upper limit at between the ages of fifteen and eighteen, and thereafter remains fixed for life, but in my own case I have shown that to be false. At the age of eleven I was given an IQ test that showed my IQ to be at the lower end of normal. Later I decided that that I was not going to be limited by other people's perceptions of my abilities and I set myself the seemingly impossible (for me) target of gaining membership of Mensa. To that end I worked to improve my mind continuously. I discovered how learning can make physical, chemical and electrical changes happen inside my brain. I noticed that if I persisted at any task for long enough, it eventually became easy. I deliberately took night-school classes in subjects that I found impossibly difficult, until I mastered them. I studied the greatest books ever written, and I learned from great thinkers who had, and still have a lot to teach me.

When, at last, I achieved my goal of becoming a Mensan, I realised that if we ignore the limits others would put on us, the only limits on our achievements are those which we impose ourselves. Whatever you score in the tests in this book, do not accept the results as final. It is my hope that this book will be the first step for many to discover their hidden potential and begin the never-ending journey of self-improvement. The trip is most certainly worthwhile.

John Bremner

Test Preparation

Many factors influence the results we achieve in IQ tests, and over the years since IQ tests were first introduced we have learned that some of those factors can have a very significant effect. The way we prepare for tests can affect our IQ score by as much as 15 points. That 15 points can seriously affect our future. The cut-off point for many jobs that test before entrance is 115. Score one point below that, and you will not even be selected for interview. But score 10 or 15 points more and you could beat other applicants for the job and be marked for rapid promotion. Employers who test for IQ are aware that the difference between bright and very bright employees can mean the difference between profit and loss for them. Similarly, some colleges use IQ tests as part of the selection process, and these tests have been shown to be more effective at selecting candidates who will do well than any other method of selection, including selection by qualifications.

If you really want to obtain the best possible IQ score that you are capable of, you need to do a bit of *MENTAL P.T.*

M **Mental alertness and mental endurance.** You are clearly going to obtain a better score if you are mentally alert than if your senses are dulled by lack of sleep or the effects of overindulgence in alcohol or food, so ensure that you get plenty of sleep before sitting a test. Be aware that the time of day can influence your score. Most people obtain their best results before noon.

E **Emotional well-being and attitude.** It is impossible to perform at peak when undergoing emotional or psychological stress. Thoughts that have nothing to do with the tests will intrude to break your concentration. You can't concentrate on a test when you are worried about how you are going to pay the mortgage. Hence, to get the best IQ score possible, it is necessary to deal with personal problems first. Make a list of everything that needs doing, and work through the list one item at a time until you have a clear life, and a clear conscience. Easier said than done perhaps, but you will feel better for having made the effort.

N **Nutrition.** A well-balanced diet with plenty of fresh fruits, nuts, legumes and vegetables is good thinking food. It is worth noting that many of the best thinkers the world has known have been vegetarians. If you can afford vitamin supplements, go for as much variety as you can obtain. Many people find that a cocktail of A, B complex, C, and E, with Ginseng and Selenium is effective at sharpening.

T **Test practice and sophistication.** Put simply, the more tests you do, the better you get at doing them. After completing the tests in this book, especially if you go back over any that you got wrong and learn from your mistakes, your IQ will be between 8 and 10 points better than when you began the tests. At this stage the increase will be temporary, but it can be made permanent if you continue your exploration of IQ tests and permanently imprint your mind with the knowledge and skills required to complete the tests.

A **Attitude.** You will obtain a better score if you are determined to do so. Get into the mood and know that you are going to perform at your best. We generally fulfil our own expectations of ourselves.

L **Learn how to relax properly.** Most people begin to lose their mental edge after doing a task for about 30 minutes, but after a break of only a few minutes you can be back to peak. Thus it is worthwhile taking advantage of any rest periods. Frequent short rests are far better for maintaining peak than working for two or three hours without a break and then stopping for a long break. Ensure that you really relax when you rest. It is surprising how many people think they are resting when they are sitting with tensed jaw and neck, with a head full of buzzing thoughts. When you do sit a test, you need to be physically relaxed but mentally focused on what you are doing.

P Physical fitness and general state of health. Studies at Manchester University have shown that the difference in IQ score between the same person tested when extra-fit, and when very unfit can be as much as 20 per cent. So if you are unfit now, a very effective way to increase your IQ score is by getting fit. Further to this, an immediate 'wake up' effect can be realised indulging in some mild exercise before sitting a test. Take a jog round the block, or do a few minutes aerobics. At the very least take a dozen fast deep breaths – the brain is a greedy consumer of oxygen. Warning – consult your doctor before beginning indulging in exercise.

T The 'Mozart' Effect. Studies have shown that listening to music for about 15 minutes before a test can have the remarkable result of temporarily increasing our IQ potential by up to 15 points. Although there are conflicting reports about the effects and the best type of music to use, the music appears to stimulate the neurones responsible for solving problems to work at peak efficiency. In my own tests I've found that complex, fast paced, classical music *which you enjoy* has the best results, and is best listened to for around 15 minutes at medium volume, on a personal stereo. The boost will be less if you have taken all the other factors into consideration.

It has been shown that, although you will gain the maximum benefit by taking all the *MENTAL P.T.* factors into consideration, there is an overlap effect. It is unlikely that you will be able to collect the maximum boost from all of them.

Test Instructions

- To provide the best possible estimate of your IQ, don't turn to the test pages until you are ready to start. Otherwise you will invalidate the result.
- Choose a quiet, well lit place where you will not be disturbed during the test. Unplug or switch off your phone.
- Have a few sheets of paper for rough working, and two or three pencils ready.
- Don't write on this book if you intend to retake the test later. Instead, jot the question numbers and your solutions on a separate sheet. (Allow yourself an extra 30 seconds per test for this.)
- Few people will complete the tests in the time allowed, so don't panic if you appear to be running out of time. You could still get a good score. For best results, once you commence the test, have a quick look at each problem, and do those that you find easiest first. If you've time left at the end of the test you can go back to the difficult ones.
- Read the questions carefully. Failure to do this is one of the main causes of wrong answers.
- The answers section contains explanations of each solution. If you went wrong anywhere, learn from your mistakes before trying another test.
- Note that the time limits on each test should be strictly adhered to. Otherwise, everyone would have a high IQ, because anyone can do the problems given sufficient time. Ideally, set an accurate alarm clock to go off when your time is up.
- If you cheat, you are fooling yourself at the expense of self-knowledge.

Warm-up Test

Before you commence any test in this book, complete this warm-up to get your mind up to speed. If you really can't do any of them, after trying your hardest, turn to the clues at the end of this test, and then try again.

Bear in mind that logical conclusions may be drawn from absurd propositions. You must accept the given facts and draw conclusions only from those facts. For example: All pictures are doormats. I have a picture. Therefore I have a doormat. (True/False)   Answer = True.

There is no time limit, but work as fast as you can.

1. Pick the odd-one-out.

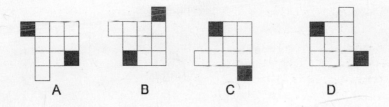

A   B   C   D

2. Underline the answers that are *closest* to being correct.

     a. The square root of 120 is (11, <u>10</u>, 12, 10.5)
     b. (50 plus 90 minus 30) divided by 2 is (52.5, <u>53.5</u>, 56.6, 57)
     c. 2x3x4x5x6x7x8 is (250, 2500, <u>25000</u>, 250000)
     d. If apples cost 6 credits, and 6 apples and 2 oranges cost 47
        credits, oranges cost (<u>6</u>, 4, 3, 2) credits.

3. If yellow bolts cost more than blue screws or white rivets, and white rivets cost less than blue screws or red nuts, and blue screws cost less than red nuts, and red nuts cost less than yellow bolts, put the items in order of cost, with (A) as the most expensive.

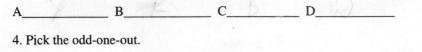

A_____ B_____ C_____ D_____

4. Pick the odd-one-out.

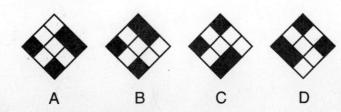

A   B   C   D

5. Which two shapes below make a pair?

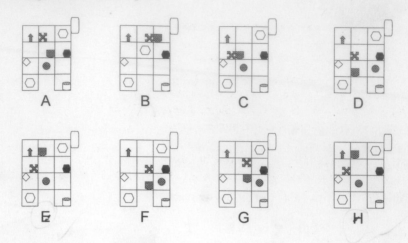

6. Find in this wordsquare, at least four fish, and a bird: (words may be in any direction, including backwards and upwards diagonals)

```
I  P  J  F  I  F  G  T  E  H  G  P  J  N  W
Y  A  T  C  Y  K  Y  O  S  M  F  N  G  L  L
R  P  I  N  E  K  C  I  H  C  F  H  W  F  T
H  P  F  J  S  F  C  U  G  H  O  P  T  W
Q  W  Q  C  Q  G  A  O  T  A  B  L  U  E  F
X  P  R  S  O  V  G  D  L  O  A  R  F  Y  Q
H  U  L  D  A  Z  A  I  H  I  B  X  R  X  H
I  K  A  W  R  L  B  W  C  O  H  D  O  C  H
X  S  H  U  X  U  M  E  T  Q  G  G  R  L  K
C  U  A  B  T  B  R  O  A  C  H  E  O  B  F
S  R  D  A  V  V  V  F  N  S  P  E  Y  P  L
M  V  D  S  C  T  Q  T  P  L  M  A  E  R  B
X  E  O  P  I  K  E  E  K  H  M  Z  L  I  C
Z  S  C  R  X  M  Z  B  T  U  O  R  T  L  D
I  I  K  Y  Z  Z  V  D  I  N  A  R  U  D  D
```

7. Underline the word in brackets that is *closest* in meaning to the given word.

Example: clock (alarm, time, <u>watch</u>, pendulum, face)

    a. spin (twist, curve, turn, round, swing)
    b. halt (wait, hesitate, abandon, terminate, start)
    c. justify (recreate, explain, decide, choose, deliberate)
    d. reserved (unwilling, taciturn, excellent, informal, friendly)
    e. declared (overt, ulterior, covert, hidden, undisclosed)

8. State whether the following *conclusion* is true or false.
All calculators are butterflies. All pigs are butterflies. All butterflies are calculators. Therefore all calculators are pigs. (T / F)

9. Insert the missing numbers.

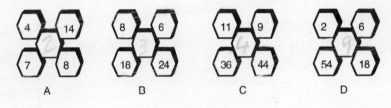

    A   B   C   D

10. This is a mirror-image puzzle. Pick the odd-one-out.

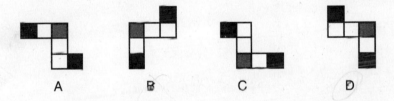

    A   B   C   D

Clues and solutions to warm-up test overleaf

Clues to Warm-up Test

Don't look at these unless you have tried your best to find the solutions first.

1. Look for mirror-image reversal.

2. a. Multiply each number by itself, and choose the one which gives the closest solution.

   b. Add 50 + 90 – 30, then divide by 2 and choose the closest solution.

   c. Find the result of 2 x 4, then multiply that by the next number, and so on, until you find the result. Rough calculations will do to give the closest solution.

   d. Work out the cost of the apples, and subtract that from 47. You will then know how much it costs for 2 oranges.

3. Write down one item to begin with, and put the others above or below it according to the information provided.

4. All the shapes are the same, but rotated, except for one which is a mirror image of the others. Find that one.

5. One of the pair is E.

6. The bird is a common domesticated egg provider. Also look for any of the following fish: COD, DOGFISH, PLAICE, SALMON, TROUT, ROACH, RUDD, PERCH, PIKE, BREAM, HADDOCK, TURBOT, HALIBUT.

7. Try putting the words into the same sentence as the given word. In most cases the solution then becomes apparent. For example, 'I can tell the time with a clock. I can tell the time with a watch. I can't tell the time with a time, an alarm, a pendulum, or a face.' The solution must therefore be watch.

8. Ask yourself, 'If c=b, p=b, & b=c, does c=p?'

9. Ask yourself, 'What do I have to multiply or divide these numbers by, to get the numbers diagonally opposite?'

10. Look for mirror image reversal.

Solutions to Warm-Up Test

1. C (mirror-image).

2. a. 11, b. 53.5 (closest to 55),

   c. 25000 (closest to 40320) d. 6 (closest to 5.5).

3. A. Yellow bolts,   B. Red nuts,   C. Blue screws,   D. White rivets.

4. B (mirror-image).

5. E & H.

6. You could have found any of the following fish, and a CHICKEN:

COD, DOGFISH, PLAICE, SALMON, TROUT, ROACH, RUDD

PERCH, PIKE,   BREAM, HADDOCK, TURBOT, HALIBUT.

7. a. turn, b. terminate,   c. explain,   d. taciturn,   e. overt.

8. False.

9. a. 2, b. 3, c. 4, d. 9.

10. D.

IQ Test 1 begins overleaf

Read the test instructions on page 14 before beginning the test.
Do not turn the page until you are ready to begin.

Test 1, Part I – Visual-Spatial

10 MINUTES

1. Which of the following shapes make two matching pairs?

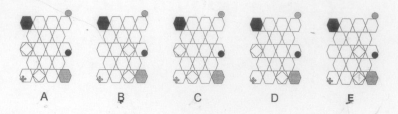

A   B   C   D   E

2. Draw a continuous line to show the shortest possible way through the maze.

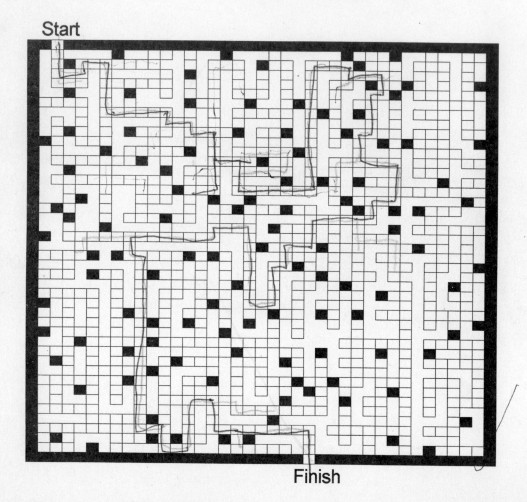

3. How many bricks are missing?

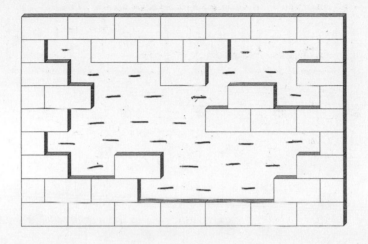

4. Decide which shape, A, B, C, or D, is the unfolded hexagonal box

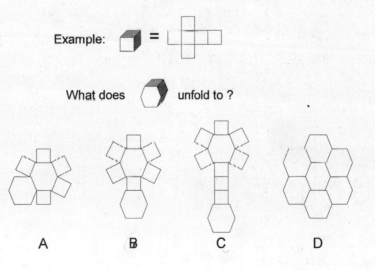

A   B   C   D

5. Circle the odd-one-out.

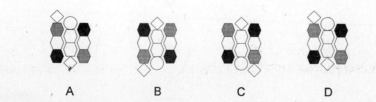

A   B   C   D

6. Circle the odd-one-out.

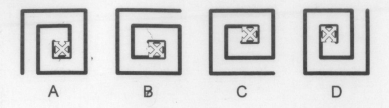

7. Which figure, A, B, C, or D, completes the analogy?

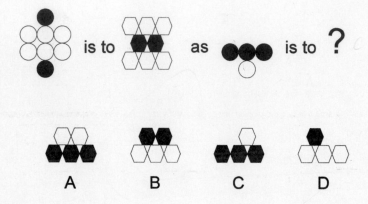

8. This is a mirror-image problem. Circle the odd-one-out.

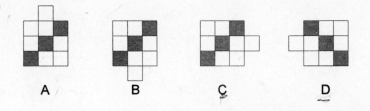

9. Which tile, A, B, C, D, E, or F, is required to complete the pattern?

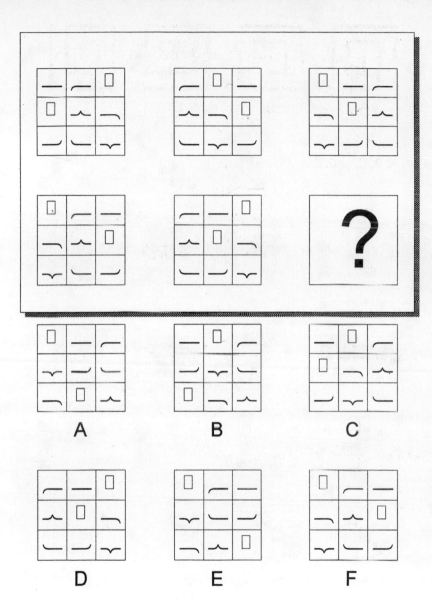

10. Some of these are mirror-image problems. Circle the odd-one-out from each set.

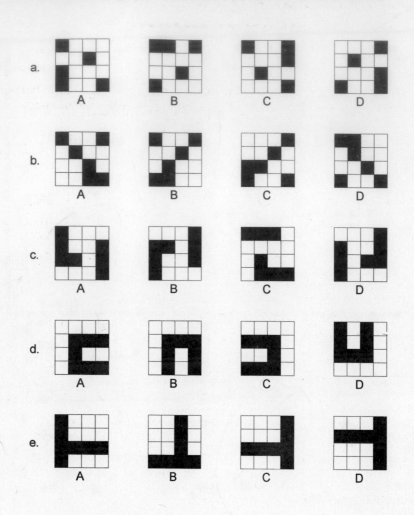

Part II – Verbal-linguistic

30 MINUTES

1. Find six of the following twelve fruits in the wordsearch puzzle. Words can be found in any straight-line direction, backwards or forwards, including diagonals, but without gaps.

APPLE   PEACH   GRAPE   AVOCADO   KIWIFRUIT   MELON
PEAR   ORANGE   PLUM   FIG   CHERRY   BANANA

```
T M A O C Z E L T Q Q B I W
F Q K I W I F R U I T T R L S
U W Q I G M F Q S W X B S W
T D C H X R M V B G U Y Q V
C I U Y M V A F I W Q D R Q
H E M F V M C P A S E G E Q
E A N A N A B N E C Z F Y P
R M W N A M O R A N G E H L
R Z Q M P G U S N X P E A R
Y E P X P V F O T C L A I R
D E J M L F L R Z V G Q H S
J F U Z E F I G S O I X K
D L T H M Q R S Y E X S C O
P G O D A C O V A P E A C H
```

2. Complete the following proverbs.

a. Ignorance is...... *is less*
b. Necessity is ...... *Mother of all invention*
c. First come ...... *First a serve*
d. Beauty is in ...... *is the eye of beholder*
e. Discretion is...... *the better part of valor*

3. Underline the odd-one-out in each group.

    a. grace, beauty, charm, care, elegance
    b. perhaps, maybe, possibly, certainly, perchance
    c. imaginary, fictional, illusory, extraordinary, hypothetical
    d. goodwill, compassion, suggestibility, benevolence, sympathy
    e. ceaseless, tiring, perpetual, persistent, interminable

4. Underline the two phrases which are closest in meaning.

    a. When one door shuts, another opens.
    b. Strange are the ways of God to man.
    c. Every cloud has a silver lining.
    d. Desire for peace, but prepare for war.
    e. Make hay while the sun shines.

5. Underline the correct subjects to match with the collective names.
Example: barren of (monkeys, geese, <u>mules</u>, doves)

    a. paddling of (ducks, seagulls, children, otters)
    b. leap of (dogs, frogs, leopards, athletes)
    c. skulk of (swine, skunks, snakes, foxes)
    d. exhaltation of (sparrows, larks, poultry, chorists)
    e. clamour of (rooks, bears, woodpeckers, housewives)

6. In each of the following, underline the two words that are nearest to opposite in meaning:
Example: <u>fast</u>, gone, space, hurry, <u>slow</u>

    a. alive, rigid, bent, round, flexible
    b. control, return, flippant, floppy, earnest
    c. agitate, calm, ridicule, confuse, stir
    d. flawed, correct, right, perfect, scratched
    e. consider, regard, hurt, insult, respect
    f. biased, naive, fair, stupid, unusual
    g. erroneous, failure, true, trick, illusion
    h. recline, dwindle, repose, relax, prosper
    i. affect, effect, quell, decline, deride
    j. exactly, roughly, tough, strictly, securely

7. Find the letters which complete the first and begin the second words of each pair.
Example: br...(anch)...or, to make *branch* and *anchor*.

    a. rever.....................................   ....ute
    b. st ....litude
    c. exa.....................................   ....ral
    d. gela ....y
    e. retr ....ion
    f. prot ....oplasm
    g. cor.....................................   ....ure
    h. dissu...................................   ....pt
    i. bra.....................................   ....ular
    j. deb.....................................   ....otto

8. In each of the following, underline the two words that are nearest to the same in meaning:
Example: <u>break,</u> alter, disturb, <u>smash</u>, twist

    a.   accumulation, reservoir, river, tryst, quarry
    b.   deceit, confusion, artifice, truth, illusion
    c.   astonish, delight, frighten, daze, amaze
    d.   guzzle, nuzzle, abstain, retreat, fast
    e.   hate, goodbye, valediction, welcome, conclusion
    f.   idol, fan, effigy, appearance, face
    g.   attitude, calmness, equanimity, agitation, uncertainty
    h.   excel, surplus, achieve, quantity, surpass
    i.   repugnant, delightful, loathsome, nice, evil
    j.   resent, accept, begrudge, fear, want
    k.   co-ordinated, arranged, synchronised, co-operated, convinced
    l.   erotic, esoteric, abstruse, psychic, ionic
    m.   dilettante, enlarge, dilate, shrink, partner
    n.   automatic, independence, ideal, autonomy, alone
    o.   pace, celebrity, package, celerity, clarity
    p.   permeate, intrude, pervade, persuade, mask
    q.   unique, sectarian, parochial, cosmopolitan, new
    r.   choice, conclusion, conjecture, diagnosis, hypothesis
    s.   protagonist, protractor, enemy, antagonist, enema

9. Find the prefixes that, when placed before each of the following groups of letters, will create valid words. Each set of words has a different prefix.
Example: –d, –coon, –conut, –cky, –ercion, become cod, cocoon, coconut, cocky, coercion, with the prefix co–.

    a. –sh, –rt, –stle, –nk
    b. –ght, –ers, –nth, ant
    c. –ject, –laze –le, –ort
    d. –ch, –con, –n, –ker
    e. –une, –ude, –ig, –ong
    f. –ss, –op, –ng, –ck
    g. –ke, –ir, –id, –dy
    h. –ory, –m, –sis, –se
    i. –aw, –all, –are, –ib
    j. –l, –st, –t, –f

10. Underline the odd-one-out from *confusion*.

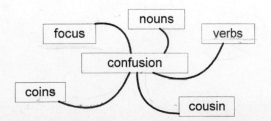

Part III – Numerical Skills

40 MINUTES

1. Find the missing numbers.

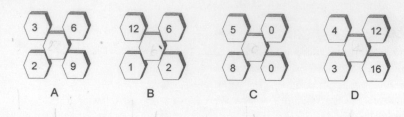

A   B   C   D

2. What comes   next in this numerical series ?

46, 30, 22, 18, (16)

3. If one banana and 3 apples cost 21 credits, and 3 bananas cost 9 credits, how much are apples?

4. Insert the missing numbers.

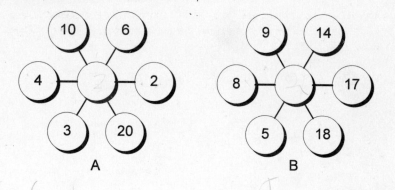

A   B

5. Insert the missing numbers.

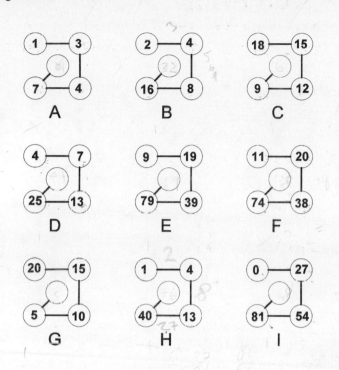

6. If black balls are worth 3, and white balls are worth 4, what is the minimum number of black balls and white balls that need to be added to make the system balance? Note: you can add black and white balls to the either side.

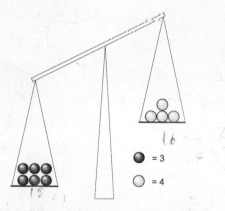

7. Halfway from your home to the office you know that you have travelled 12km. If you turn around after going a further 4km, and head back home, then travel for a further 6km before changing your mind again and heading back to the office, then again change your mind after travelling for 5km, how far will you have to travel to get back home?

8. Adding the numbers as you go, find a route from one of the shaded hexagons at the top of this puzzle, to one of the shaded hexagons at the bottom, that gives 100 as a total. Landing on a zero or on any numer next to a zero, or next to a black hexagon, reduces your score to zero.

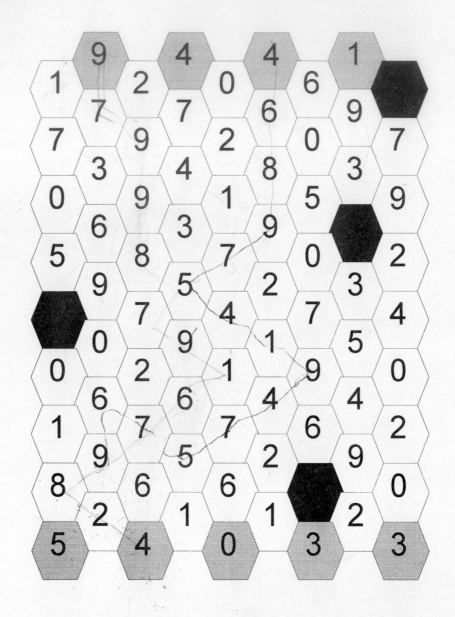

9. Which tile comes next, A, B, C, D, E or F ?

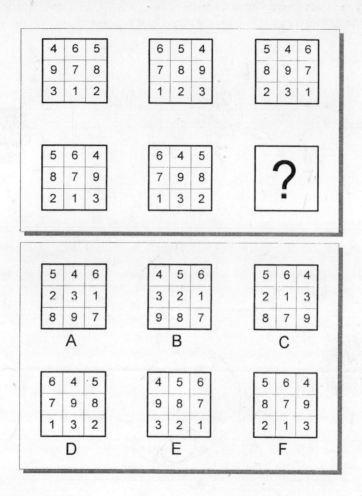

10. Complete these analogies.

      a. 144 *is to* 12 as 3 *is to* 9 as 64 *is to* (   )
      b. 50 *is to* 2.5 as 100 *is to* 5 as 20 *is to* (   )
      c. 3 *is to* 48 as 2 *is to* 32 as 4 *is to* (   )
      d. 5 *is to* 26 as 8 *is to* 65 as 7 *is to* (   )
      e. 3 *is to* 34 as 4 *is to* 46 as 5 *is to* (   )
      f. 12 *is to* m as 4 *is to* e as 2 *is to* (   )

Part IV – Logic

●●●●●●●●●●●●●●●●●●●●●●●●●●●●●●●●●●●●●●

25 MINUTES

1. Is the following *conclusion* true or false?
      All dogs are blue with red hair. All dogs are peanuts. All peanuts
   are blue with red hair, therefore all peanuts are dogs.

2. Ann has three chocolates, one of which she knows has been poisoned. Which of the following can she say for certain?

   a. If I eat all of these chocolates I will get ill.
   b. If I eat two of these chocolates and I don't get ill, the remaining chocolate will be the poisoned one.
   c. If I eat all of these chocolates and I die, I will know that the poison was very toxic.
   d. If I don't eat any of these chocolates I will remain healthy.
   e. If I drop all of these chocolates in water and one of them floats, I will know that it has been poisoned.
   f. If I taste all of these chocolates, I will be able to tell which one has been poisoned by the flavour.
   g. I'd be safer not to eat any of these chocolates.
   h. I can safely eat two of these chocolates.
   i. Cyanide smells of almonds. This chocolate smells of almonds, therefore this chocolate is poisoned with cyanide.
   j. The person who gave me these chocolates intended me harm.

3. Find the missing total.

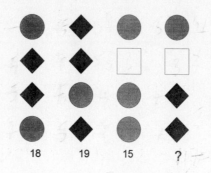

   18   19   15   ?

4. Underline the odd-one-out.

   a. seeing : view
   b. smelling : scent
   c. touching : object
   d. hearing : sound
   e. tasting : food

5. Complete each analogy by underlining the correct word.
Example: car is to travel as sit is to (eat, relax, <u>stay</u>, walk, bend)

     a. aunt is to niece as mother is to (child, son, daughter, girl, cousin)
     b. door is to house as gate is to (timber, garden, hinges, lock, open)
     c. hand is to throw as gun is to (powder, bullet, barrel, kill, shoot)
     d. high is to low as above is to (over, under, below, down, low)
     e. asleep is to dormant as awake is to (active, yawn, stretch, stand, quiet)

6. Which of the figures below, A, B, C, or D, matches the figure in the box?

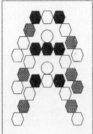

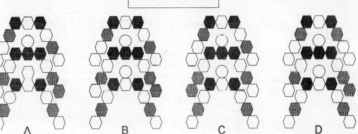

   A   B   C   D

7. Is the following *conclusion* true or false?

All windows are feathered. All computers are sneezes. Some mammals are fire-engines. Some windows are computers. Therefore some sneezes are feathered.

8. If red is worth more than blue, and yellow is worth more than green and orange, but less than blue, and orange is worth less than green, put the colours in the box below according to their value, with 5 as the highest.

1	Orange
2	Green
3	Yellow
4	Blue
5	Red

9. Since BLACK = 1 and CHICKEN = 14, insert the missing value.
    TRAFFIC = (   )

10. Five people have to share the use of a pink chair, a black chair, and a red chair. Donna will sit only on a red chair, and shares it with James alone. Linda shares only with James and Mary. Alan will sit only on a pink chair, and shares it with Mary alone. Assuming that all who use the chairs use them for sitting on, state which of the following conclusions are true (T), false (F), or possible but not certain (P)

        a. Mary sometimes sits on a red chair.
        b. James sometimes sits on a black chair.
        c. Alan likes Mary.
        d. Donna, James and Linda sometimes share the same chair.
        e. James and Mary share a chair.
        f. Linda likes the colour black.
        g. Mary can sit on a pink chair or a black chair.
        h. Linda only sits on a black chair.
        i. James likes both Linda and Donna.
        j. They need more chairs.

Part V – Creative Ability

●●●●●●●●●●●●●●●●●●●●●●●●●●●●●●●●●●●●

We are all born with a certain amount of creative ability, but in some people that ability remains latent, while in others it is developed and enhanced. It is also possible that you may be creative in ways that are quite unique. Since creative people, on the whole, tend to have higher IQs than uncreative people,[3] or to put it another way, those with higher IQs tend to be more creative than those with lower IQs, it seems fair to suggest that if you have a high level of creative ability, your IQ will have more value than an equivalent IQ rating of someone with low creative ability. Having the potential to create with your intelligence must be better than having 'dormant' intelligence. Thus, the score for the creative tests will make a contribution to your final IQ score.

Practice

If it were not true that creativity can be enhanced with practice we would be unable to learn expression in music or art. As with so many other skills, the best way to develop our creativity is to is to *try* to do so. Most creative hobbies are inexpensive – all you need is a pencil and a sheet of paper to write poetry, or a box of water-colours and a sheet of paper to paint. For the cost of a hamburger you can buy a lump of clay to sculpt. For the cost of a drink you can buy a harmonica, or an old guitar at a car-boot sale. You may never know that you have a talent unless you explore the possibilities. Just think – what if Mozart had been brought up in a house without music, or if Einstein had never been given the little book on Euclid's geometry that sparked his interest?

Satisfaction

The more areas of creativity we work on, the more we enhance our all-over creative abilities, and the more satisfaction and enjoyment life brings us. Some of the most satisfying moments we have are when we can stand back and look at a finished project – something we have fashioned on our own, and say, 'I made this with my own hands. It was hard going, but it was well worth the effort.'

For those who have the courage to take a step into a totally different lifestyle, there is no better way to earn a living than doing something creative that you enjoy and getting paid for it.

It needs to be pointed out that many highly intelligent people are not particularly creative because their creativity is stifled by their work. Mature left-brain thinking is required in most jobs for dealing with correspondence, adding figures, making practical decisions, and giving and taking orders. Creative thinking is a skill that uses the right-brain's immature ability to visualise and conceptualise. If you can think like a child again, you can begin to be more creative.

Here is what some other people have to say about creativity:

> "When in doubt, make a fool of yourself. There is a microscopically thin line between being brilliantly creative and acting like the most gigantic idiot on earth. So what the hell, leap."
> *Cynthia Heimel*

---

[3] There is a correlation of around +0.5 between creativity and intelligence, which means that there is a 50% chance that if you are more creative than average, you will also be more intelligent than average, and vice-versa.

"Quiet and activity are the opposite sides of creative energy. I doubt that anyone can ever be a creative activist who is not at the same time a creative quietist."

Dr Norman Vincent Peale

"The uncreative mind can spot wrong answers, but it takes a creative mind to spot wrong questions."   *Anthony Jay*

Concrete and fluid creativity

Creativity is difficult to measure in written tests. Some of the problems have an unlimited number of possible answers to the problems, and there are may be no 'closed' answers that can be marked right or wrong. There is no objective test that can rate a piece of music or writing, or sculpture, and the measure of the value of ideas is entirely subjective.

The creativity problems that follow contain a mixture of open and closed tests which should give an estimate of both *concrete* creativity (relating to learned skills and creative problem solving) and *fluid* creativity (relating to ingenious flexibility).

Don't waste time with detail. The object in each test is to achieve maximum originality and variety.

30 MINUTES

1. Write down 20 uses for a common brick.

(handwritten answers)
Build a house
Build a Wall
Brick a window
BALANCE on HEAD
See if it can Float as sinks
Decorate the Brick paint
Paper Weight
Door Stop
Exercise with Biceps
Hammer T Nadale with
throwing weight
stepping stone

_____

_____

_____

_____

_____

_____

2. This large cube is made up of 64 smaller blocks which are stacked. What is the least number of blocks you would have to remove to rearrange the stack into another perfect cube?

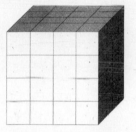

3. Find the name of a famous wartime leader and political figure by solving the following anagram: (Clue – middle name has 7 letters)

chroniclers swept in lunch

4. Find twenty valid English words derived from the word *creativity*. You may only use letters the same number of times they appear in the original word. Words of 5 letters or more score 1 point. Words of 4 letters or less score half a point.

Example: activity, reactivity, cavity, tar

5. How many different hands of two cards is it possible to make from the four cards below?

6. As part of a test you are given a key to this room and told that inside you will find two ropes hanging. Your task is to grasp both of these ropes, but you find that you can't reach one without letting go of the other. How can you complete your task?

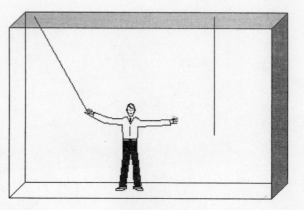

7. Can these boxes be arranged into a solid cube? (Yes / No)

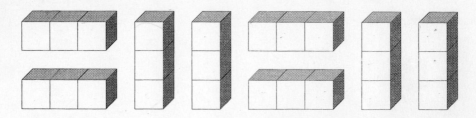

8.

Use this 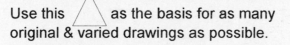 as the basis for as many
original & varied drawings as possible.

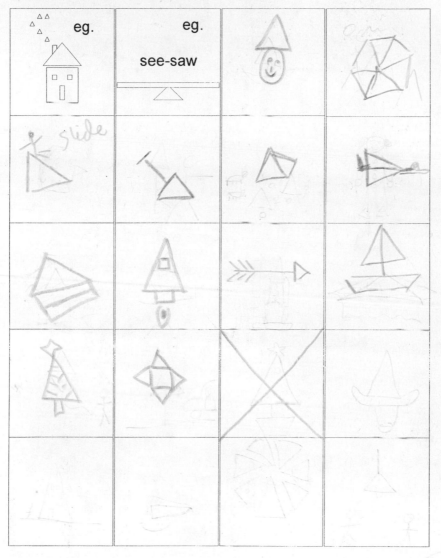

"It is not enough to have a good mind; the main thing is to use it well."
Rene Decartes

9. Quickly read down the list of colours, *looking at the word* on each line and reading aloud, as quickly as you can, whether the object *really is* striped, checked, dotted, black, grey or white. You get ten points for this if you read the list fluently without mistakes, but you lose a point for each error or definite pause, so note down your number of mistakes at the bottom of the page. (10 seconds maximum allowed)

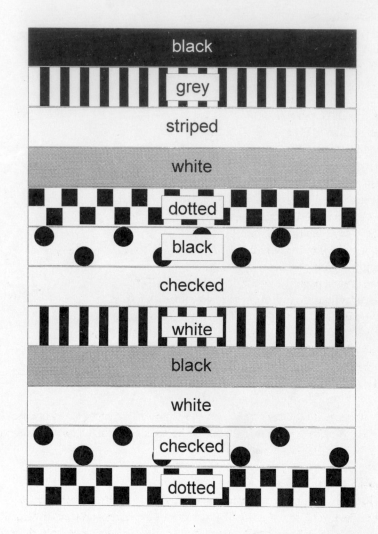

Number of pauses or mistakes_____0_____

10. Complete this short creativity questionnaire. Be honest with yourself. Circle true (T), false (F), or uncertain (U).

     a. I'm good at thinking up new ideas. (T/F/U)
     b. I'm good with my hands. (T/F/U)
     c. I have designed and made things which I own. (T/F/U)
     d. People ask me for my ideas. (T/F/U)
     e. I get paid to think. (T/F/U)
     f. I do my own decorating. (T/F/U)
     g. I enjoy creative writing. (T/F/U)
     h. I have a natural flair for art. (T/F/U)
     i. I enjoy experimental cooking. (T/F/U)
     j. I have sold things which I have made. (T/F/U)
     k. I get paid to make things. (T/F/U)
     l. I dislike jobs without an end-product. (T/F/U)
     m. I have the urge to create. (T/F/U)
     n. I can play a musical instrument. (T/F/U)
     o. I have a flair for languages. (T/F/U)
     p. I am good at solving complex problems. (T/F/U)
     q. People say I have a good imagination. (T/F/U)
     r. I'm a good actor or mimic. (T/F/U)
     s. I enjoy solving puzzles (T/F/U)
     t. I can draw a passable likeness of a person. (T/F/U)
     u. I am adventurous and enjoy new experiences. (T/F/U)
     v. I draw fascinating doodles while on the phone. (T/F/U)
     w. I often think of new and better ways to do things. (T/F/U)
     x. I enjoy reading fiction. (T/F/U)
     y. I can easily amuse myself. (T/F/U)
     z. I can make up new jokes that make people laugh. (T/F/U)

Creative ability tests are difficult to score, since for some of the problems there are no right and wrong answers and each idea or drawing needs to be considered on its merits, so before you turn to the answers, please read the guidelines below.

Scoring the creative tests

For each truly different idea or useful drawing, score one point. Better still, get someone else to score you on this. As a very rough guide, if you stuck to the time limits and managed around 30 total points, you don't seem to be highly naturally creative, but you could still do well in closed tests with definite answers, and you are certain to have other abilities that will prove useful. We are all good at something. A score of around 50 is about average – you have the potential to improve and develop your creativity to a useful level. If you scored over 75, you are more creative than average, and should be able to make good use of that creativity to enhance your lifestyle. With a score closer to the maximum possible, you are highly creative and will probably feel unfulfilled if you do not find a regular outlet for that creativity. If you have not already done so, find a medium for self-expression.

Creativity score summary:

89 to 100	– gifted
76 to 88	– very creative
63 to 75	– good creative skills
50 to 62	– average creative skills
31 to 49	– slightly below average creative skills
30 or lower	– potential to improve

Your score for this test, together with the other three *less open* creative tests in this book, contributes to your overall IQ score using one of the scoring options.

This concludes IQ Test 1. Turn to page 111 for answers and marking details, then turn to page 109, where you will find details of how to convert your scores to an IQ rating.

You will achieve a better score if you take a break before starting IQ Test 2.

••

IQ Test 2 begins overleaf

••

Read the test instructions on page 14 before beginning the test.
Do not turn the page until you are ready to begin.

Part I – Visual-Spatial

18 MINUTES

1. Which two of the following cards make a matching pair?

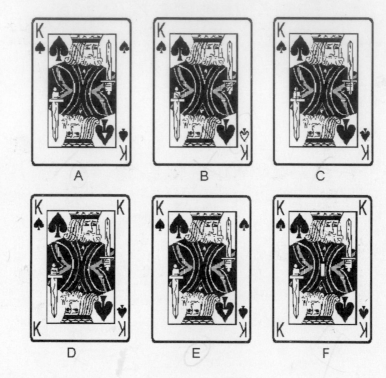

2. This is a mirror-image puzzle. Pick the odd-one-out.

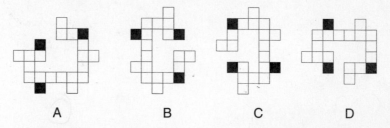

3. Another mirror-image puzzle. Pick the odd-one-out.

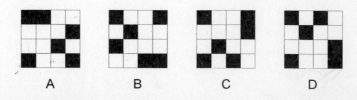

4. Find the missing shape.

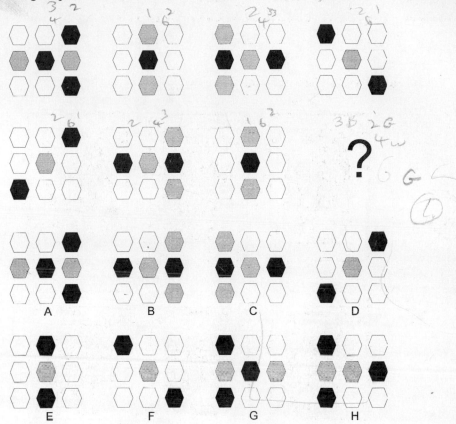

5. Complete the analogy.

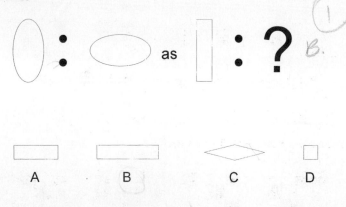

6. All except D are mirror-image puzzles. Pick the odd-one-out from each set.

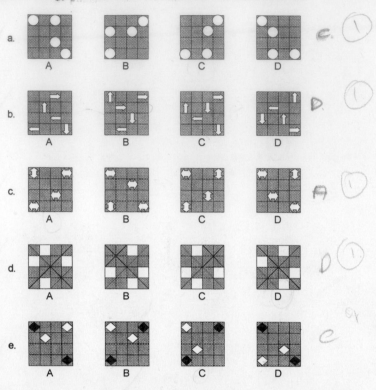

7. Complete the analogy.

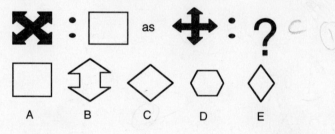

8. How many bricks are missing?

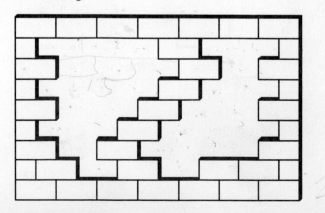

9. Pick the odd-one-out.

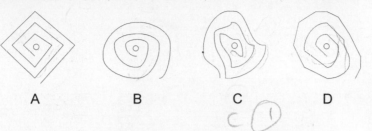

A   B   C   D

10. Using the rules that you may not land on 2 consecutive white hexagons, and you may not go back to a hexagon that you have already been on, mark the route from A to B that allows you to collect as many diamonds as possible.

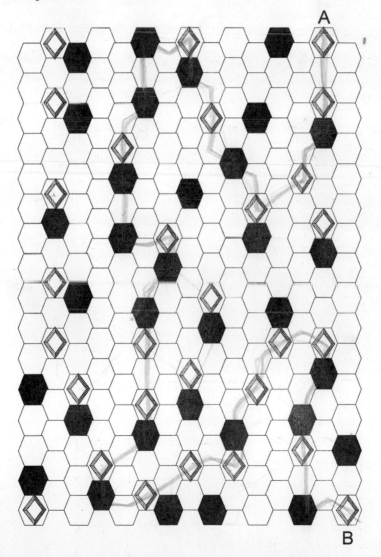

Part II – Verbal-linguistic

40 MINUTES

1. Pick the odd-one-out. Clue: fish

a. bithaul   b. loudfern   c. hergrin
d. howlfibs   e. culttee   f. harks

2. Fill in the missing words in the following sentences by choosing from the words below each sentence.

a. The ....why rivers and seas ....the homage of a hundred mountain ....
is that they keep ....them.   – *Lao Tzu*
decision, beating, streams, reason, give, conclusion, below, receive, lions, above, fish, men, drowning

b. Every .... girl knows about .... It is only her .... to .... for
it that increases.   – *Francois Sagan*
puppy, girl, female, love, algebra, insane, refusal, hope, suffer, little carpentry, capacity, duty,
delight, dog, love, capacity, person, pay, die

c. We have genuflected before the .... of .... only to find that it has given us
the .... bomb, producing fears and .... that science can never ....
                                                      – *Martin Luther King*
statue, illusion, delights, god, fears, science, old, yesterday, mitigate, nasty, electric, unique,
bastard, atomic, producing, confusion, master, anxieties, give

3. Complete each analogy.

Example: satisfy *is to* craving as eat *is to* (hunger, swallow, food, bite)

a. much *is to* plethora as few *is to* (none, any, modicum, excess, part)
b. joke *is to* laugh as pain *is to* (hurt, cry, overcome, injure, sore)
c. rest *is to* relax as survive *is to* (sleep, thrive, exist, eat, hunt)
d. hand *is to* foot as finger *is to* (palm, digit, nail, heel, toe)
e. lute *is to* musician as hammer *is to* (break, carpenter, knock, thump, nail)

4. In each of these sentences, underline the word or group of words in brackets which makes the sentence *most generally* true.

Example. A cup is for (water, beans, liquid, coffee, tea)

        a. A woman is (clever, attractive, childbearing, female, young)
        b. Dogs are (prone to biting, domesticated, canine, lazy, greedy)
        c. Bang is (a firework, a retort, a thunderclap, noise, a crash)
        d. A car is (noisy, smelly, going somewhere, transport, metal)
        e. Houses are (castles, comfortable, warm, homes, weatherproof)
        f. Diamonds are (beautiful, clear, expensive, on rings, gems)
        g. Concrete is (messy, building material, heavy, solid, wet)
        h. Breakfast is (early, after sleep, ham and eggs, welcome, food)
        i. Wealth means (happiness, freedom, jealousy, money, parties)
        j. An uncle has a (nephew, brother, niece, sibling, wife)

5. Complete the following proverbs.

a. The labourer is... Worthy of his hire, many hands
b. Boys will be... Boys
c. Cowards die... many times
d. There's many a slip... twixt cup ships
e. There's many a good tune... played on an old fiddle

6. Find the letters which complete the first and begin the second words of each pair.
Example: pre...(judge)...ment, to make *prejudge* and *judgement*.

        a. com. FORT ....itude
        b. cul. VERT ....igo
        c. har. VEST ..... VEST ibule
        d. con. CURR ....rent
        e. bul......... ....ess
        f. flot......... ....ple
        g. count...... ....on
        h. pro......... ....let
        i. en............ ....ry
        j. de............ ....worthy

7. a. Find a route from the top to the bottom of this puzzle that takes you through enthusiasm, smelly, and yellow. Words can overlap. As an example, the word potential is shown.

b. Which letter of the alphabet has not been used?

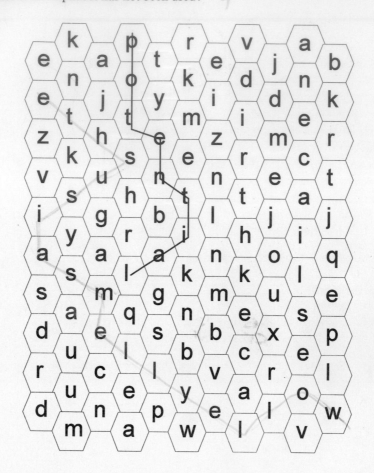

8. Underline the two words in each set that do not go with the other words.

Example: lion, leopard, <u>rabbit</u>, <u>bear</u>, jaguar

a. lettuce, parsnip, cauliflour, spinach, carrot
b. brick, rock, boulder, concrete, stone
c. camera, photographer, model, lens, flashbulb
d. bottle, decanter, jug, crystal, silver
e. yes, affirmative, go, okay, proceed
f. bite, lick, nibble, chew, suck
g. tree, batten, plank, beam, wood
h. within, around, inside, throughout, interior
i. haphazard, designed, helter-skelter, random, organised
j. mock, abhor, taunt, deride, despise

9. Circle the odd-one-out from *meditation*.

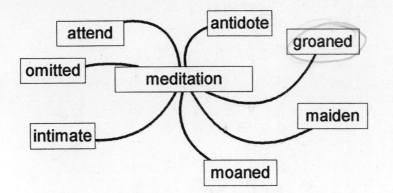

10. Solve the following anagrams. (They make single words)

Example: Pure Elvis (crush*)* (Solution – *pulverise*)

    a. hot rages (deficit) .... *shortage* ....
    b. large hut (mirth)..................................
    c. red ale (commander)........ *leader* ....
    d. rotate fun (lucky)........ *fortunate* ....
    e. a spider (give up in sorrow)........ *despair* .....
    f. mere squalor (belligerent)..............................

Part III – Numerical Skills

40 MINUTES

1. Insert the missing numbers to make all the columns, rows, and long diagonals of these tiles add to 15, without repeating a number on the same line.

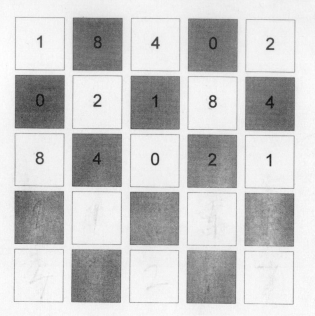

2. Complete these analogies.

Example: 12 *is to* 47 as 4 *is to* (   ). Solution = 15 (1 less than 4 x 4)

        a. 9 *is to* 81 as 7 *is to* (   )
        b. 110 *is to* 11 as 14 *is to* (   )
        c. 28 – 12 *is to* 8 as 34 – 20 *is to* (   )
        d. 3 x 9 + 24 *is to* 17 as 3 x 15 + 15 *is to* (   )
        e. 12 + 18 – 10 *is to* 2 x 40 as (3 x 12) + 4 *is to* (   )

3. Circle the odd-one-out in each row.
This is not simply a matter of choosing odd and even numbers.

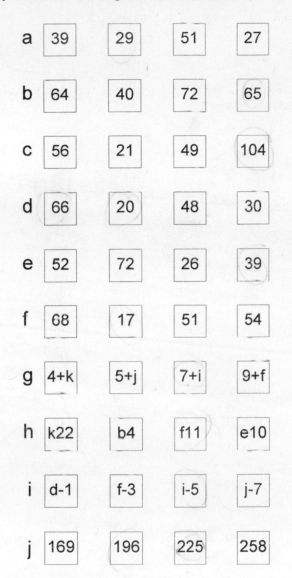

a 39   29   51   27

b 64   40   72   65

c 56   21   49   104

d 66   20   48   30

e 52   72   26   39

f 68   17   51   54

g 4+k   5+j   7+i   9+f

h k22   b4   f11   e10

i d-1   f-3   i-5   j-7

j 169   196   225   258

4. a. What number gives 12 when you multiply it by 3 and divide by 11?
   b. What number gives 15 when you divide it by 6 and add 11?
   c. What number gives 34 when you multiply it by 2 and subtract 6?
   d. What number gives 30 when you multiply it by 15 and subtract 60?
   e. What number gives 7 when you multiply it by 2 and divide by 10?

5. Insert the missing numbers.

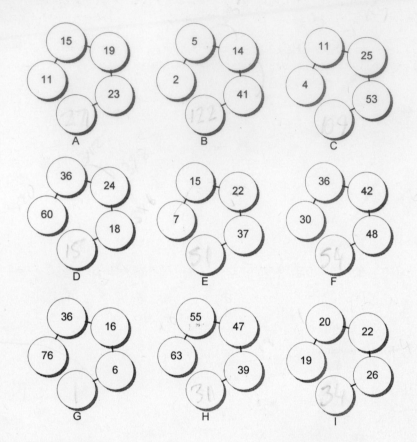

6. Supply the missing numbers.

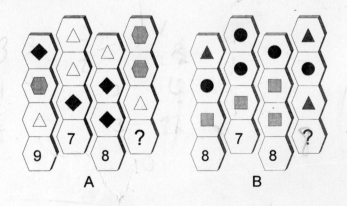

7. a. If you were to draw straight lines between the homes of Yvonne, Scott and Juan, below, who all live in Eldorado, what would be the area enclosed by the lines, in square kilometres?

b. If it takes Yvonne half-an-hour to get to Scott's house, what would her average speed be over the journey?

c. If Juan and Scott both set off for point x at the same time, but Juan travels at 80 kilometres per hour and Scott travels at 150 kilometres per hour, who would get there first?

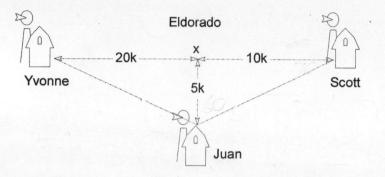

8. If 2 peaches and 1 avocado cost 10 credits, and 2 avocados and 1 peach cost 8 credits, how much each are:

    a. avocados?

    b. peaches?

9. Insert the missing numbers.

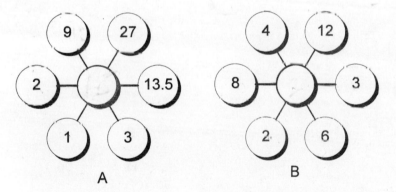

A   B

10. Monday = 3, Tuesday = 5, Wednesday = 7, Thursday = 9, Friday = 11, Saturday = 13, and Sunday = 15.

a. If today is Wednesday, what is the value of the day before the day after tomorrow?

b. If three days from now will be the day before the day that is worth 13, what is the value of today?

c. If the day after tomorrow is worth 15, what day will be two days before the day before yesterday?

d. If today is worth 13, what is the total value of the day after tomorrow, plus the day that is two days before the day after the day after tomorrow?

e. If yesterday was Tuesday, what is the total value of the day after the day after tomorrow, plus the day before the day after yesterday, plus the day after tomorrow?

Part IV – Logic

37 MINUTES

1. On a shelf in Conchita's house there are five ornaments, a lion, a tiger, a spotty dog, a miniature statue of liberty, and a stone totem-pole. From the observer's point of view the spotty dog is two to the left of the totem-pole. The lion is two to the left of the spotty dog. The totem-pole is to the right of the statue of liberty. The spotty dog is immediately to the left of the statue of liberty. Put the ornaments in their correct order from left (a) to right (e).

a_____

b_____

c_____

d_____

e_____

2. State whether the *conclusion* is true or false.
All razors are bananas. All hi-fi systems are egg-timers. Some egg-timers are razors. Some pencils are hi-fi systems, therefore some bananas are egg-timers.

3. By giving alpha–numeric values to consonants and vowels, work out:
   a. If Jack is worth 1, and Minnie is worth 23, what is David worth?
   b. If Ken is worth 14, and Bill is worth 12, what is Liz worth?
   c. If Roald is worth 16, and Annie is worth 15, what is Nan worth?
   d. If Graham is worth 9 and Felix is worth 20, what is Basil worth?
   e. If Ivan is worth 46, and Adam is worth 19, what is Abdul worth?

4. Using the key provided, decode the message below it.

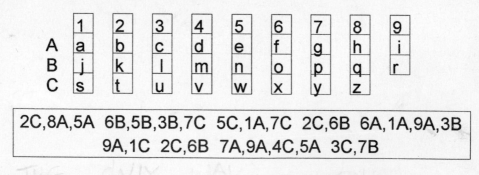

	1	2	3	4	5	6	7	8	9
A	a	b	c	d	e	f	g	h	i
B	j	k	l	m	n	o	p	q	r
C	s	t	u	v	w	x	y	z	

2C,8A,5A 6B,5B,3B,7C 5C,1A,7C 2C,6B 6A,1A,9A,3B
9A,1C 2C,6B 7A,9A,4C,5A 3C,7B

5. Which card is the odd-one-out?

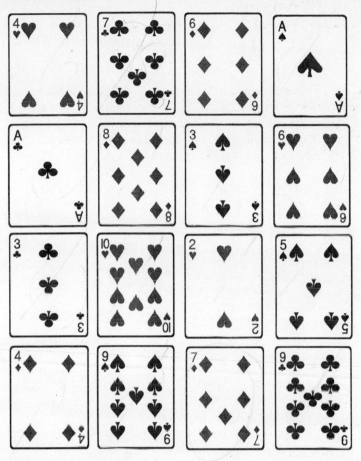

6. State whether the *conclusions* in the statements below are certainly true. If not certainly true, they are false.

    a. My father and brothers drink a lot, therefore I drink a lot.

    b. All puppies are good. I have a puppy, therefore it is good.

    c. Some glasses are fish. Some newspapers are fish. Therefore some glasses are newspapers.

    d. There are more odd vowels in the alphabet than even vowels.

    e. Celia has a big stick, therefore she is dangerous.

7. Insert the missing letters or numbers in the boxes provided.

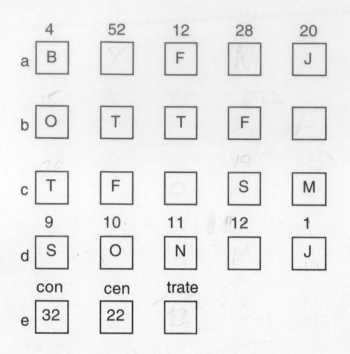

	4	52	12	28	20
a	B		F		J

b	O	T	T	F	

c	T	F		S	M

	9	10	11	12	1
d	S	O	N		J

	con	cen	trate
e	32	22	12

8. Suzanne has two black hats and one green hat. Bobbie has one red hat and one hat the same colour as the hats that Mary has three of, and two hats the same colour as the hat that Suzanne has one of. Mary has three yellow hats, and two hats the same colour as the hats that Suzanne has two of. They have no other hats than those mentioned. State whether the following statements are true (T), false (F), or possible, but not necessarily true (P).

    a. Bobbie has most hats.
    b. Neither Bobbie, Mary, nor Suzanne prefer red hats.
    c. There are more black hats than any other colour.
    d. Bobbie has a yellow hat.
    e. Suzanne has a hat the same colour as one of Bobbie's hats.
    f. Mary has two black hats.
    g. Neither Bobbie, Mary, or Suzanne need so many hats.
    h. Between them all they have thirteen hats.
    i. Bobbie, Mary and Suzanne are friends.

9. In the below panel you may slide a counter in either direction onto a blank square or you may jump over a single different coloured counter onto a blank square. Using only those two rules, how many moves does it take to get the black counter to the other side of all the grey counters?

10. Referring to the diagram below, if 'a' moves in a clockwise direction, what direction do each of the other cogs move in – clockwise (C), or anticlockwise (AC) ?

b_____   c_____   d_____

e_____   f_____   g_____

h_____   i_____   j_____

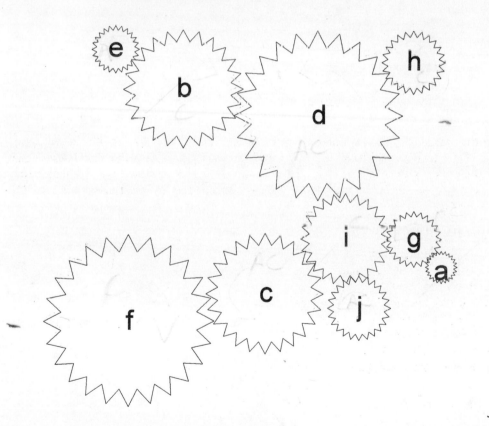

Part V – Creative Ability

20 MINUTES

1. How can you bridge the gap between the top of these walls using only the two short wooden planks and the saw? Draw the solution.

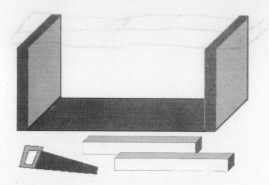

2. Write down 20 words that rhyme with *ash*.

SASH, LASH, MASH HASH BASH CASH
DASH, GASH, RASH VASH BALDERDASH
VHITEVASH,

3. You are in a locked cupboard that hasn't been opened for years. You are hungry and thirsty, and the door is bolted from the outside. You got in there on your own, but you can't get out and nobody can hear you shouting or banging on the door. How did you get in there?

4. List 16 ways to get six feet off the ground.

5. You are in an long narrow enclosed room with a wooden batten, and a banana hanging on a string, and nothing else. When you place the batten against the side walls, it is too steep to climb. When you place it against the end walls, no matter what angle you use, you can't quite reach the banana. If you jump you will break your neck. How can you reach the banana to untie it from the string?

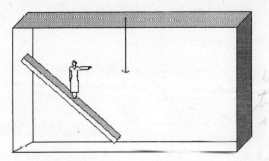

6. You have just fallen stark naked 50 metres out of a window. Beneath the window is a pile of jagged rocks. You have not hurt yourself. How did you achieve that?

7. You have a cup containing milk, and a cup containing an equal quantity of water. If you take a spoonful of the water and put it into the milk, then stir thoroughly, and then take a spoonful of the milk and put it into the water and stir thoroughly, is there now (a) more water in the milk than milk in the water, or (b) vice versa, or (c) neither?

8. You have to travel to a friend's house in your car. Your car has no fuel, and none is to be had. Nevertheless, you get into your car and do the trip without assistance. How did you get there?

9. How can you calculate the height of a tree from the length of its shadow, using only a measuring stick?

10. List 20 original ways to boil an egg.

For example : Fire it from a gun and boil it by air friction.

Turn to page 42 for scoring information on the creative tests.

This concludes IQ Test 2. Turn to page 115 for answers and marking details, then turn to page 109, where you will find details of how to convert your scores to an IQ rating.

You will achieve a better score if you take a break before starting IQ Test 3.

••

IQ Test 3 begins overleaf

••

Read the test instructions on page 14 before beginning the test.
Do not turn the page until you are ready to begin.

Part 1 – Visual-Spatial

15 MINUTES

1. These are mirror-image problems. Circle the odd-one-out in each row.

2. Complete the analogy:

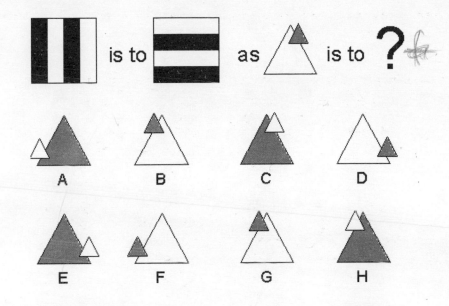

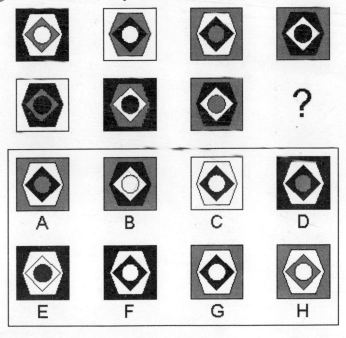

3. Pick the missing tile from those in the panel below.

4. Which of the solutions below should replace the question mark?

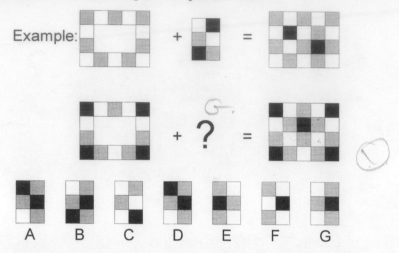

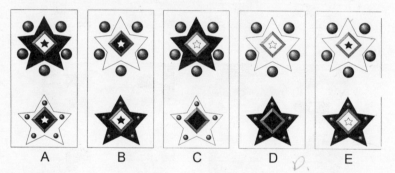

5. Pick the odd-one-out from the following shapes.

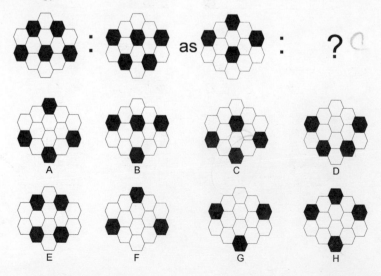

6. Complete the analogy.

7. Which shape continues the sequence?

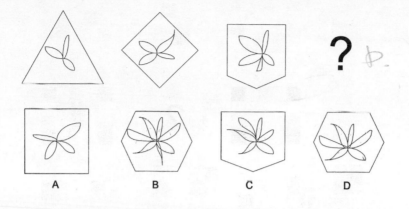

8. Some of these are mirror image problems. Circle the odd-one out in each row.

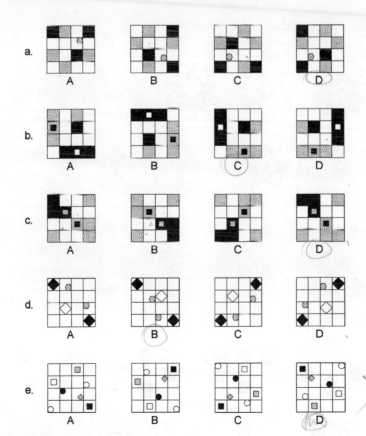

9. Decode the following message:

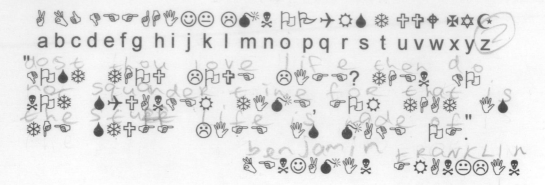

10. Which tile comes next?

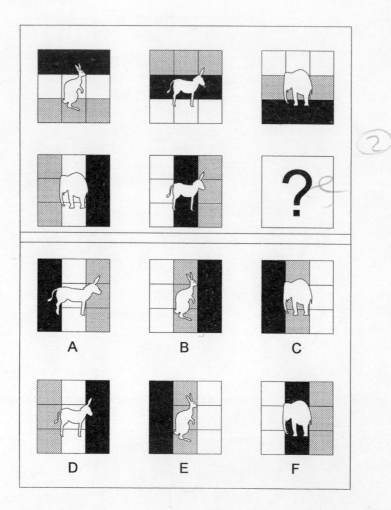

Part II – Verbal-linguistic

45 MINUTES

1. Find the letters which complete the first and begin the second words of each pair.

Example: w...(alk)...ali, to make *walk* and *alkali*.

a. carp *et* .... *et* ..hnic
b. her.....................   ....erman
c. f ....ion
d. psy ....ory
e. scho ....ch
f. bo *vine* .... *vine* .gar
g. fru ....lant
h. glim .... .udo
i. sequ ....ated
j. cir.....................   ....ver

2. Complete the following proverbs.

a. A watched pot...
b. A rolling stone...
c. A penny saved...
d. All roads.... ....
e. Dead men...

3. Underline the odd-word-out in each line.

   a. dextrous, deft, adroit, inept, facile
   b. instructive, didactic, educative, verbose, pedagogic
   c. isolate, ignore, boycott, exclude, extrude
   d. temperate, dissolute, libertine, debauched, lewd
   e. evaluate, ratify, endorse, certify, validate

4. Solve the following anagrams. Each anagram makes a single word which is the name of a type of animal.

   a. skelter (bird of prey)..
   b. raptor (good mimic)..
   c. niphold (sea mammal)..
   d. lunar tata (spider)..
   e. toe riots (slow mover)..

    f.   radio mall (armour plated)..

    g. coke cap (proud bird)..

    h. Arab slots (sea bird)..

    i.   cool cider (river terror)..

    j.   a cellar trip (food for some, pest to others).....................

5. Insert the missing letters to make suitable words. Each dash stands for a letter.

    a. A word that means *stage* – j _ _ _ _ _ re

    b. A word that means *stumble* – f _ _ _ er

    c. A word that means *squeeze* – c _ _ _ _ ss

    d. A word that means *resolute* – s _ _ _ _ _ rt

    e. A word that means *stately* – a _ _ _ _ t

    f.   A word that means *torpid* – s _ _ _ _ _ sh

    g. A word that means *danger* – j _ _ _ _ _ dy

    h. A word that means *incurable* – t _ _ _ _ _ l

    i.   A word that means *heavenly* – b _ _ _ _ _ _ l

    j.   A word that means *crux* – n _ _ _ _ _ s

6. In each of the following, underline the two words that are nearest to the same in meaning:

Example: <u>heartless</u>, murderous, considerate, <u>callous</u>, stupid

    a. inapt, stupid, inarticulate, inappropriate, suitable

    b. heap, burden, work, handicap, collection

    c. docile, submissive, arrogant, tired, terrified

    d. error, precondition, element, flaw, fallacy

    e. corrupt, ugly, bland, chaste, pure

    f.   release, detain, extricate, proclaim, insert

7. Find the prefixes that, when placed before each of the following groups of letters, will create valid words. Each set of words has a different prefix.

Example: –ry, –nch, –stion, –ll, become query, quench, question, quell, with the prefix que–.

    a. –sp, –nt, –pple, –in

    b. –ing, –ip, –ident, –ike

    c. –mmy, –mp –ng, –im

    d. –rt, –t, –se, –sten

    e. –am, –ast, –aker, –nign

    f. –ound, –ort, –rupt, –ove

    g. –ch, –rful, –se, –m

    h. –e, –ity, –se, –ge

    i. –ck, –nch, –ath, –ak

    j. –lk, –g, –nd, –ot

8. Complete each analogy.

Example: coffee *is to* drink as bread *is to* (dough, <u>eat</u>, birds, flour)

   a. look : eyesight as listen : (aware, ear, hearing, sound, noise)
   b. foreigner : alien as local : (newcomer, native, immigrant, earth, spaceman)
   c. crucial : critical as trivial : (lazy, pursuit, danger, matter, unimportant)
   d. cruelty : barbarity as mercy : (live, war, compassion, execution, hospital)
   e. normal : usual as atypical : (same, different, symbolic, chosen, ideal)
   f.   boorish : oafish as polite : (refined, crude, clever, brave, cruel)
   g. straight : ordinary as wry : (smart, dry, droll, wheat, daring)
   h. volatile : erratic as constant : (steady, always, unique, wild, slow)
   i. amenable : intractable as : vacillating (uncertain, unequivocal, concluding, inoculation, unsteady)
   j. tough : hard as perfidy : (loyalty, treachery, love, hate, friendship)

9. Insert the missing words, choosing from the list below each sentence.

a. There are few things _____ in themselves; it is the _____ to achieve them that we _____ more than the means.   *Francois, Duc de la Rochefoucauld*

ridiculous, need, lack, money, delight, impossible, application, tough, alone, have

b. With our actions, we _____ our most deeply held _____ and beliefs, and through the global _____ of our mass media, even the _____ actions we take have the power to influence and _____ people of all nations.

             Anthony Robbins

infer, actions, vomit, ridiculous, send, money, values, contact, move, biggest globulation,communicate, influence, simplest,

c. Most of us have no adequate _____ of our inherent powers and _____. At heart, we _____ ourselves. We do not really _____ in ourselves and for that reason remain weak, _____, even impotent, when we could be strong, _____, victorious.   *Dr. Norman Vincent Peale*

collection, concern, powers, dominate, conception, know, dominant, abilities, see, unconscious, unusual, ineffectual, reflect, underestimate, believe, wild

d. It is the _____ of genius to confer a measure of itself upon inferior intelligences. In reading the works of Milton, Bacon, and Newton, _____ greater than the growth of our own minds are transplanted into them; and feelings more profound, _____, or comprehensive are _____ amidst our ordinary train.   *James Montgomery*

unity, day, hope, protruding, reading, prerogative, insinuated, found, minds, thoughts, perfidious, sublime, invaded, greatness, inheritance, human, unusual, stuck, focused

10. Find six of the twelve items of cowboy's equipment, plus an item of underwear that is not standard cowboy equipment.

BEDROLL	CHAPS	HOLSTER
SPURS	LASSO	REVOLVER
SADDLE	RIFLE	BULLWHIP
STETSON	HORSE	NECKERCHIEF

```
B L G S K A G I R G I G O K I G O
E E O J F I G K A O K A L A U K U
A F D B A J A S G I G E G R S R A
K O G R S O G U E R N G S G U G S
S G G A O U G J G E E L D D A S U
A I I S A L A E A T U V A R U B I
F A G S U O L A S S O I O O U N O
E U G I R H G R U L I G U L A G S
I M U E E R U G K O G K L I V O I
H K A R I F L E A H A W U R I E U
C U R E U G U G U U H U I G U U R
R I A I O U G A S I E O A U K E S
E G O K O K E T P U G U R G R G U
K U G U G U E A A O A K I S U G U
C A I E A T O U H A U S P U E A N
E K G U S U R G C U E U U R A U S
N U I O U I K U U R R U G G U G U
U A N U I G O I O S A E A I O K A
```

Part III – Numerical Skills

1. Insert the missing numbers.

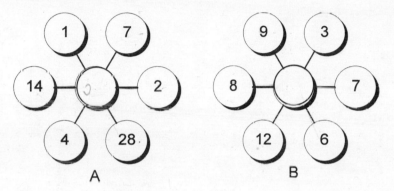

2. If two aubergines and one sweet potato costs 25 credits, and one aubergine and one sweet potato cost 19 credits, how much are:

    a. aubergines

    b. sweet potatoes

3. Insert the missing number in the blank hexagon.

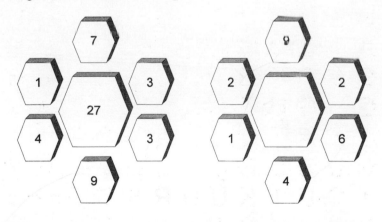

4. Insert the missing numbers.

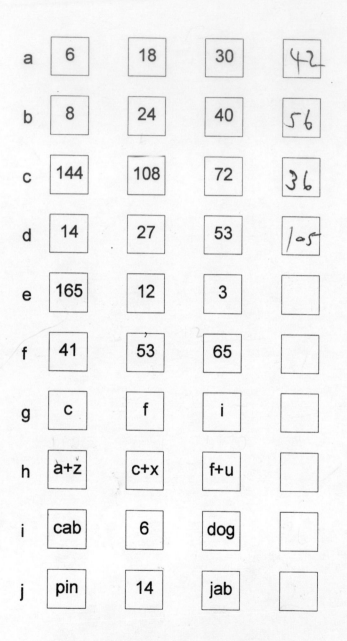

a	6	18	30	42
b	8	24	40	56
c	144	108	72	36
d	14	27	53	105
e	165	12	3	
f	41	53	65	
g	c	f	i	
h	a+z	c+x	f+u	
i	cab	6	dog	
j	pin	14	jab	

5. If you need 2 dark balls on the right to balance the scales, what is the value of the white balls.

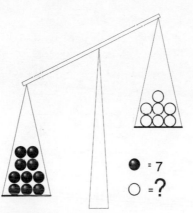

6. Work out the value of the last set in each row.

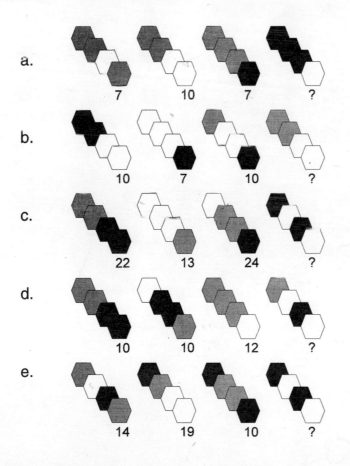

a.   7   10   7   ?

b.   10   7   10   ?

c.   22   13   24   ?

d.   10   10   12   ?

e.   14   19   10   ?

7. Geoff is half the age represented by the number of days in most Februarys. Kelly is the age that Geoff would have been six years ago if Geoff were now a year older. Derek's age can be divided by seven and by three, and is less than Hans' age. Hans is less than forty, and if he were eleven years younger he would be seven years older than Derek. Derek's age is seven times the age that Kelly would be if Kelly were only a third of the age that she is. If you divide Derek's age by three, and multiply it by four, you get Wolf's age. Work out the ages of:

      a. Geoff (   )
      b. Wolf (   )
      c. Hans (   )
      d. Kelly (   )
      e. Derek (   )

8. What number should replace each question mark?

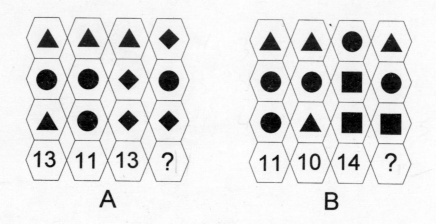

9. Arthur, Dee and Sandy live, in that order, on a long straight road. Dee lives 10km from Sandy, and 20km from Arthur.

    a. If both Arthur and Sandy set off towards each other's homes at the same time, and both travel at 30kmh how far from Dee's house will they meet?

    b. If Dee travels to Sandy's house at 60kmh, and as soon as he arrives, turns round and travels to Arthur's house at 40kmh an hour, how long will the combined trip take him?

10. Adding the numbers as you go, find a route from the top to the botom of this puzzle, that gives 50 as a total. Landing on any number next to a zero reduces your score to zero. Landing on a black hexagon halves your score.

Part IV – Logic

•••

30 MINUTES

1. What is the value of the missing total?

brick	cup	brick	cup
cup	rug	cup	cup
rug	rug	rug	cup
brick	rug	cup	rug
15	13	19	?

2. Which two proverbs are most similar in meaning?
   a. Do as you would be done by.
   b. One good deed deserves another.
   c. Everyone to his own opinion.
   d. Time is a great healer.
   e. If you want something done, ask a busy man.
   f. Procrastination is the thief of time.
   g. Nothing succeeds like success.
   h. There is no accounting for taste.
   i. It is better to be poor and happy than rich and unhappy.
   j. Let sleeping dogs lie.

3. Who is the best person to ask whether something is true or false?

   a. Someone who is occasionally truthful.
   b. Someone who is often truthful.
   c. Someone who is never truthful.

4. Using the key provided, decode the message below it.

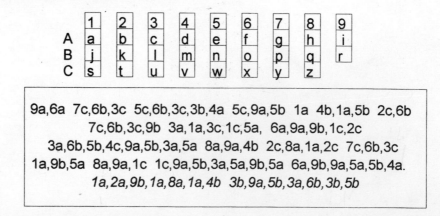

	1	2	3	4	5	6	7	8	9
A	a	b	c	d	e	f	g	h	i
B	j	k	l	m	n	o	p	q	r
C	s	t	u	v	w	x	y	z	

9a,6a 7c,6b,3c 5c,6b,3c,3b,4a 5c,9a,5b 1a 4b,1a,5b 2c,6b
7c,6b,3c,9b 3a,1a,3c,1c,5a, 6a,9a,9b,1c,2c
3a,6b,5b,4c,9a,5b,3a,5a 8a,9a,4b 2c,8a,1a,2c 7c,6b,3c
1a,9b,5a 8a,9a,1c 1c,9a,5b,3a,5a,9b,5a 6a,9b,9a,5a,5b,4a.
1a,2a,9b,1a,8a,1a,4b 3b,9a,5b,3a,6b,3b,5b

5. State whether the *conclusions* in the statements below are true or false.

a. Some yellowfish are blue. Some redfish are gold. Some goldfish are red. Some blackfish are red. Some bluefish are yellow. Therefore some blackfish are gold.

b. Some peanuts are widgets. Some widgets are bad. Some peanuts are books. All books are good. Some bananas are widgets. Some widgets are good. Bananas are neither good nor bad. Therefore some peanuts are good.

c. Some puzzles are slips. Some politicians are slips. All puzzles are liars. Some puzzles are flowers. All politicians are flowers. Therefore some politicians are liars.

d. Some jokes are blanks. Some blanks are curtains. Some pennies are curtains. Therefore some blanks are pennies.

e. Some buttons are hats. All dollars are red. Some buttons are black. All hats are red. No dollars are buttons. Therefore some buttons are red.

6. The relevant *position* of the component shapes in this puzzle is irrelevant. Pick the odd-one-out.

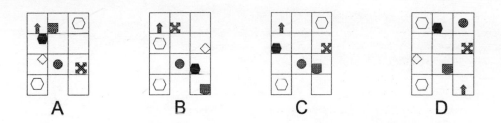

7. How can you get this straight-sided beaker exactly half full, from its current state of being more than half-full, without any measuring instruments or other containers?

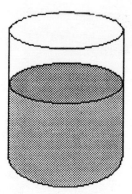

8. If it takes Wilfred an hour to dig a square hole deep enough to bury his bank manager's cat, how long will it take him to dig a similar square hole twice as wide and twice as deep to bury his accountant's dog?

9. Sandy is older than his wife Gail. John is younger than Sandy. Lorraine is Gail's younger sister. Nicola is Gail's eldest child. Gail is Sandy's wife. Colin is Nicola's brother, and Sandy's son. John, Lorraine's husband, is older than Sandy's wife. Lorna-Jane is Lorraine's oldest child. Fraser is Lorna-Jane's brother. Gail and Sandy had both of their children before Lorraine and John started their family. Lorraine is younger than John.

Put all eight people mentioned in order of age, with (a) as the oldest.

a._____, b._____, c._____,

d._____, e._____, f._____,

g._____, h._____

10. Decode the anagram in the box, using the key provided. Clue: it flies.

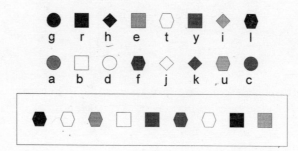

Part V – Creative Ability

•••••••••••••••••••••••••••••••••••••

40 MINUTES

1. Assuming that all blocks are supported by other blocks, work out:

a. How many blocks are in this construction?

b. Without moving any of the existing blocks, how many need to be added to this construction in order to make a larger rectangular block?

c. If you are permitted to move just one of the existing blocks, what is the minimum number of blocks that need to be added to this construction in order to make a larger rectangular block?

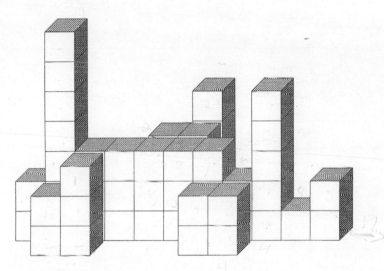

2. List 20 words that rhyme with *brain*.

_____

_____

_____

_____

_____

3. Write down 20 uses for a light bulb.

4.

Use this ◯ as the basis for as many
original and varied drawings as possible

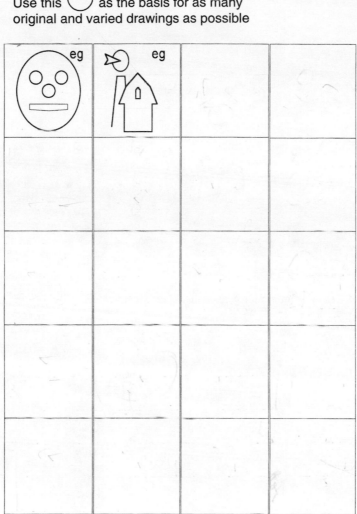

"Success comes in cans, not can'ts!" – Napoleon Hill

5. In a nuclear power plant a fifty ton flask was put on transportation rollers which measured half-a-metre around, to be moved a distance of six metres. Assuming that when a roller is freed it is placed immediately back under the front end of the flask, how many complete turns would the rollers underneath the flask have to make to move the flask the required distance?

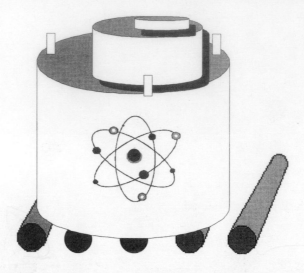

6. Draw the shortest route from corner A to corner B on the surface of this solid block.

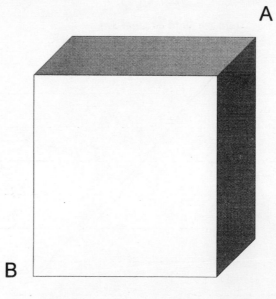

7. Rearrange these seven matches to make:

    a. 3 equal triangles.
    b. 4 equal triangles.

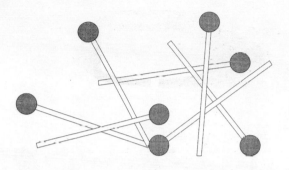

8. Circle the beaker which is the odd-one-out.

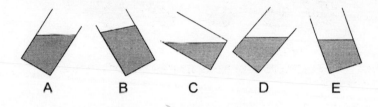

     A   B   C   D   E

9. Find twenty words derived from the word *imagination*.
Example: *animation; nation; toning*.

_____

_____

_____

_____

_____

_____

_____

_____

10. Complete the acrossword puzzle to find a word, in the third column, that defines a quality often required by creative people.

Clue	1	2	3	4	5	6
imagines						s
crave or long for	d	e		i	e	
lucky symbol				c		
small towell or bib			p			
tests		r				
marching display	p					
gratitude		h				
ringed planet			t			
plague or pestilence				g		
saggy					p	
seeker						r

Turn to page 42 for scoring information on the creative tests.

This concludes IQ Test 3. Turn to page 119 for answers and marking details, then turn to page 109, where you will find details of how to convert your scores to an IQ rating.

You will achieve a better score if you take a break before starting IQ Test 4.

IQ Test 4 begins overleaf

Read the test instructions on page 14 before beginning the test.
Do not turn the page until you are ready to begin.

Part 1 – Visual-Spatial

18 MINUTES

1. Which tile from the panel below completes the pattern?

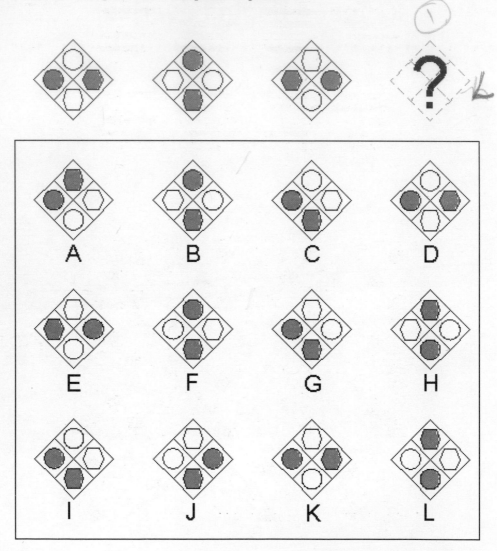

2. Complete the analogy:

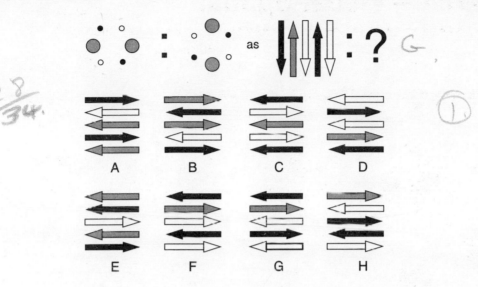

$\frac{28}{34}$

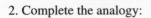

3. Choose the missing block of tiles from those below.

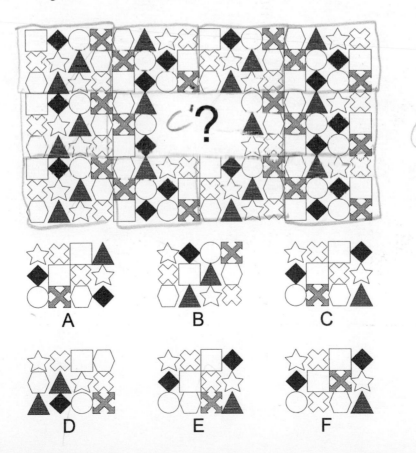

4. These are mirror-image puzzles. Circle the odd-one-out in each row.

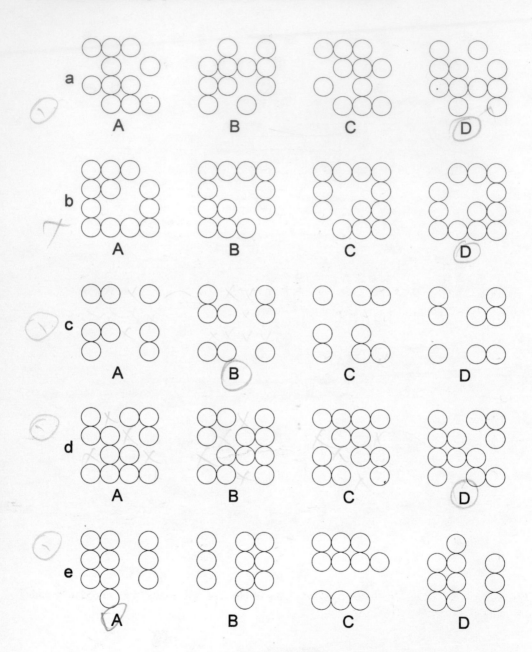

5. Circle the two shapes in each row that are rotated mirror-images of the other three.

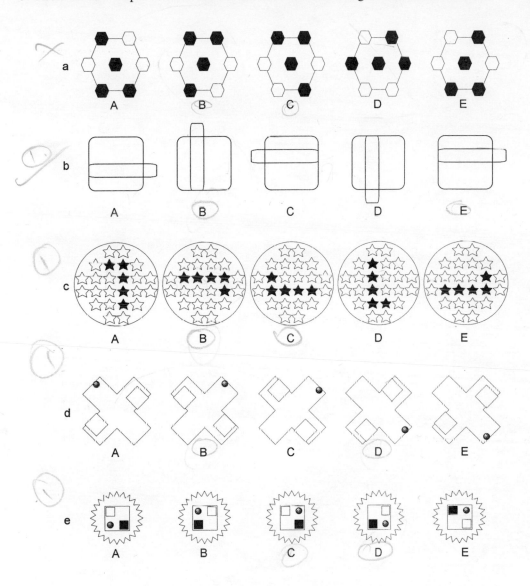

6. This system is in balance. If a block is added on top of block A, how many blocks need to be added on top of block B to stay in balance?

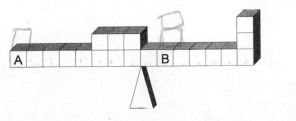

7. Complete the analogy.

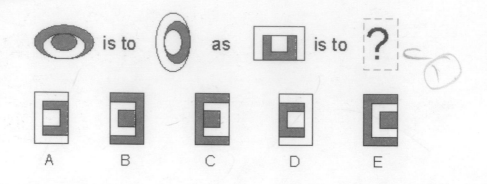

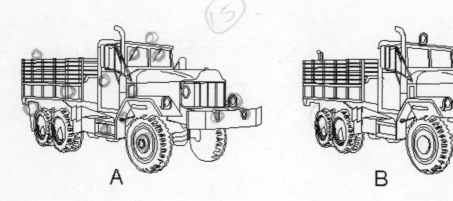

8. Circle ten differences between A and B.

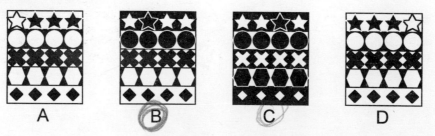

9. Which is the odd-one-out?

10. Select the missing butterfly from those in the panel below.

Part II – Verbal-linguistic

• •

45 MINUTES

1. Insert the missing letters to make suitable words. Each dash stands for a letter.

    a. A word that means *empty* – h _ _ _ ow

    b. A word that means *mix* – m _ _ gle

    c. A word that means *raid* – i _ _ _ de

    d. A word that means *exact* – p_ _ _ _ _ t

    e. A word that means *dangle* – h _ _ g

    f. A word that means *seige* – b _ _ _ _ _ de

    g. A word that means *body* – c _ _ _ _er

    h. A word that means *boast* – b _ _ _ _ er

    i. A word that means *keeper* – c _ _ _ _ _ r

    j. A word that means *gust* – s _ _ _ ll

2. Complete the following proverbs.

a. A stitch in time...

b. Better the devil you know...

c. It takes a thief..

d. In the country of the blind..

e. Little strokes..

3. Underline the odd-word-out in each line.

    a. liturgy, documentation, paperwork, forms, questionnaire

    b. corporeal, incarnate, tangible, spiritual, physical

    c. fragrance, perfume, scent, bouquet, sniff

    d. sacrilege, defilement, desecration, sacrosanct, disrespect

    e. abiding, enduring, ephemeral, eternal, immutable

4. a. What word, starting with *con* means *speculation*? (_____)

   b. What word, starting with *san* means *permit*?   (_____)

   c. What word, starting with *acq* means *accede*?   (_____)

5. Find six of the following birds, plus one cat in the wordgrid.

CROW·   CURLEW ·   EAGLE ·
FALCON ·   IBIS ·   MACAW ·
KESTREL ·   KINGFISHER · OWL ·
PIGEON ·   PARROT ·   SPARROW ·

```
P Y U Z V U F E C U E U C J Q Y
A I W C E A Z N S F B K C F Z F
R L Z T W A G F D R K G W X A N
R O E J S O P A A U K A V G Q M
O B L R P X Z L H L C W D B E O
T G V R T Y P C M A O X G L J X
J P E E L S V O M J A L G C X I
X P I C G M E N Y K E A U Z B M
O X I X S X B K A O E R Q I N E
G S H G G W N I P X L S S R A X
D N F D E V J A D E D C Z X W H
V S P U I O R H W Y R R B D N Z
L W O N D D N S F N E O V J V D
K R H X S Z X X S G F W O C K G
I M K I N G F I S H E R F E V F
O U E S P A R R O W Z D S Q A Z
```

6. In each of the following, underline the two words that are nearest to opposite in meaning.

Example: kind, sad, gender, callous, thoughtless

    a. organised, coalescent, fused, obscure, random

    b. daring, nebulous, ridiculous, goodly, clear

    c. fragile, base, error, noble, valour

    d. dialogue, rapport, conflict, disturb, hardship

    e. concomitant, meagre, attending, nominal, nimble

7. Solve the following anagrams. Each anagram makes a single word which is the name of a type of flying machine. The anagram words are not clues.

    a. logic mirth..

    b. large pony..

    c. reach for TV..

    d. triple echo..

    e. lean apes..

    f. cash pipes...

    g. rid leg...

    h. Irish pa...

    i. cert OK...

    j. lean opera...

8. In each of the following, underline the two words that are nearest to the same in meaning:

Example: cool, warm, <u>boiling</u>, <u>hot</u>, tepid

    a. lamb, flesh, bacon, meat, rump

    b. intimate, intimidate, insinuate, order, hurt

    c. validate, invalidate, violate, interrupt, abrogate

    d. inconstant, definite, bewildering, fickle, imperfect

    e. wax, wander, abate, wallow, wane

9. Find the prefixes that, when placed before each of the following groups of letters, will create valid words. Each set of words has a different prefix.

Example: –ash, –endour, –ice, –it, become splash, splendour, splice, split, with the prefix spl–

    a. –flet, –p, –ve, –rning

    b. –ief, –ibe, –eezy, –oken

    c. –rgy, –gory –viate, –ge

    d. –ggle, –the, –te, –ng

    e. –ign, –ound, –ist, –ide

    f. –rst, –ry, –y, –tt

10. Find a route from the top to the bottom of this puzzle that takes you through the statement 'All knowledge is of some value'.

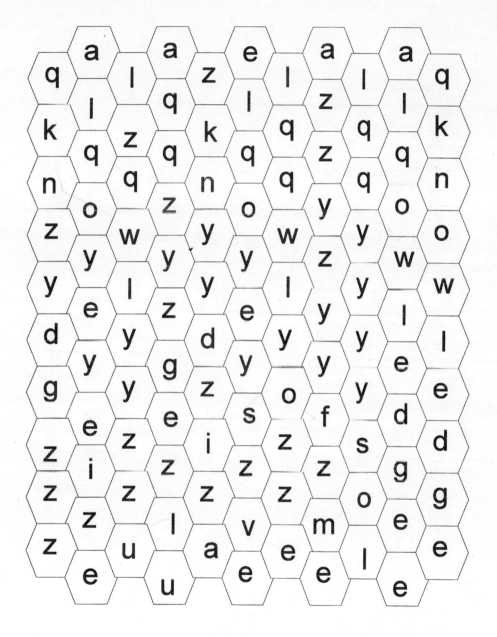

Part III – Numerical Skills

•••••••••••••••••••••••••••••••••••••

40 MINUTES

1. Insert the missing numbers in the blank boxes.

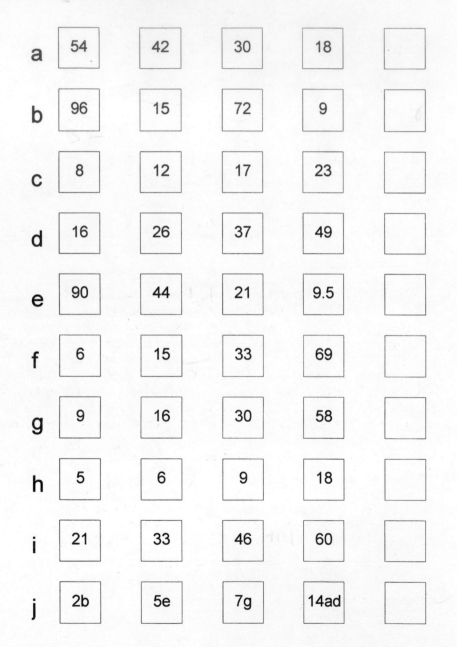

a 54   42   30   18   ☐

b 96   15   72   9   ☐

c 8   12   17   23   ☐

d 16   26   37   49   ☐

e 90   44   21   9.5 ☐

f 6   15   33   69   ☐

g 9   16   30   58   ☐

h 5   6   9   18   ☐

i 21   33   46   60   ☐

j 2b   5e   7g   14ad ☐

2. Insert the missing numbers to make all the columns, rows, and long diagonals of these tiles add to 25.

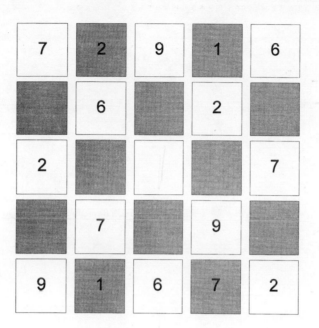

3. a. What number gives 4 when you multiply it by 3 and divide by 6?
   b. What number gives 15 when you multiply it by 8, divide by 10 and add 11?
   c. What number gives 3 when you multiply it by 7, add 6, and divide by 9?
   d. What number gives 10 when you multiply it by 2, divide by 6, and add 6?
   e. What number gives 2 when you multiply it by 3, subtract 3, divide by 6 and subtract 2?

4. a. If you are left with 75 credits after giving 4 times the cost of the barrels in change to someone who bought 5 barrels of gunge from you, how much was the gunge per barrel?
   b. If you are left with 18 credits after giving 6 times the cost of the woogets in change to someone who bought 9 woogets of splodge from you, how much was the splodge per wooget?

5. What is the missing number in the right-hand shape.

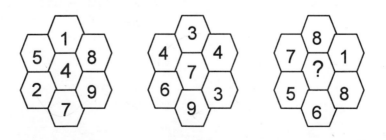

6. Work out the value of the right-hand shapes.

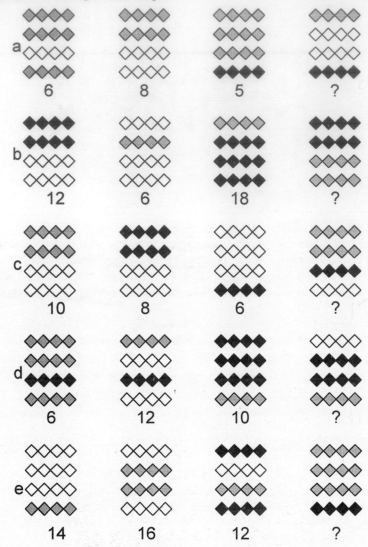

7. Insert the missing numbers in the blank circles.

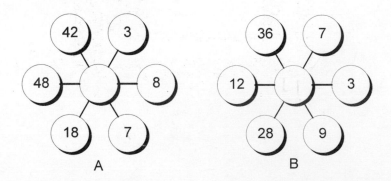

8. Work out the missing numbers.

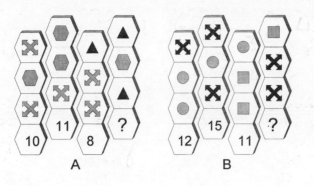

9. The value of each day remains constant from week to week.

a. If the day before yesterday was three days before Saturday, what day will tomorrow be?

b. If the day before yesterday was five days before Wednesday, what day will tomorrow be?

c. If it will be Sunday in three days, what will be the day before two days after yesterday?

d. If Wednesday is the day after tomorrow, what day was the tomorrow of the day before yesterday?

e. If Monday is worth half of Wednesday, and Wednesday is worth half of the day after five days before the day before next Thursday, which is worth 8, what is Monday worth?

10. The volume of each of the smaller boxes is half of the volume of the bigger box behind it. Using that information, determine:

a. What is the total volume of all the boxes?

b. What is the surface area of the biggest box?

c. How many times will the volume of the smallest box go into the largest box?

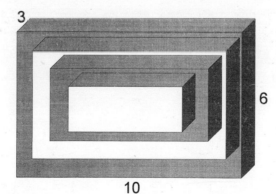

Part IV – Logic

• •

25 MINUTES

1. How many colours does it take to colour this map of America so that no two adjoining areas end up with the same colour?

2. State whether the *conclusion* in each of the following is necessarily true or false.

a. All pigs are green. All pens are blue. Some pens are pigs. Some pigs like boiled sweets. Some boiled sweets are blue pens. Therefore some boiled sweets are green.

b. All nuts are silver. All beans are blue. Some blue beans are sticky oil. Some silver nuts are blue beans. Some blue beans are forbidden books. Some sticky oil is forbidden books. Therefore some silver nuts are sticky oil.

c. All wood is dolls. All balls are black. Some dolls are white balls. Some black balls are white balls. Some black balls are purple cubes. Some purple cubes are dolls. Therefore some purple cubes are white balls.

3. Which one of the shapes below is the same as the shape in the box?

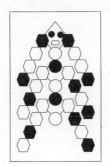

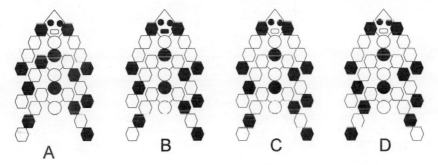

4. Complete each analogy by underlining the correct word.

Example: lacerate *is to* cut as teach *is to* (knife, school, <u>inform</u>, pupil, teacher)
 a. prime *is to* heyday as flower *is to* (scent, seedling, grow, bloom, colour)
 b. obstacle is to overcome as mountain *is to* (rock, high, sky, climb, courage)
 c. precede *is to* antecede as before *is to* (later, now, soon, previously, then)
 d. theoretical *is to* practical as pragmatic *is to* (dozy, dreamy, stupid, sensible, expert)
 e. hoax is to hoodwink as flirt is to (sex, love, friendship, tease, fool)

5. Which elephants make two identical pairs?

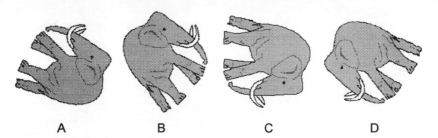

6. If both orange and green are worth more than red, but both blue and yellow are worth less than red, and if green is worth less than orange, and yellow is worth less than blue, put the colours in the box below according to their value, with 5 as the highest.

1	
2	
3	
4	
5	

7. Insert the missing letter of each sequence:

a. T, N, E, S, S, (___)

b. O, S, A, J, J, (___)

c. F, S, S, M, T, (___)

8. State whether the *conclusion* to each of the following are necessarily true (T) or false (F).

a. John hates football. All the children in the playground play football, except when it rains. None of the children play golf or basketball. All of the teachers play golf. John is a child. Therefore John plays football, except when it rains, but not basketball.

b. One hundred people ran a race. Everyone who finished the race got a medal. Anthea didn't get a medal. Jane ran the race and got a medal. Philip didn't run the race and didn't get a medal. Therefore Anthea didn't run in the race.

c. The pyramid inside this block takes up half of the volume of the block.

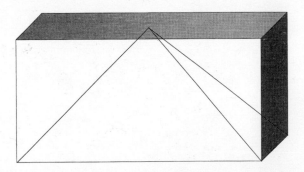

9. Which sets of cables could be removed safely without the system of suspension for this clock collapsing?

     a. A, C & D (Essential/Non-essential)
     b. B, C & D (Essential/Non-essential)
     c. C & A (Essential/Non-essential)
     d. D & B (Essential/Non-essential)
     e. A, B & C (Essential/Non-essential)

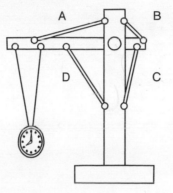

10. Looking at the system of cogs below, determine:

     a. If D turns clockwise, does J turn clockwise (C) or anti-clockwise (AC)?
     b. If L turns anti-clockwise, does Q turn clockwise (C) or anti-clockwise (AC)?
     c. If E is turned with a certain force, will it require a greater (G) or lesser (L) force than the force applied to E to prevent J from turning?

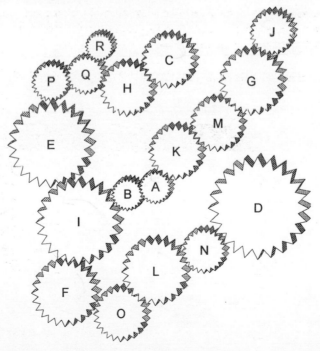

Part V – Creative Ability

25 MINUTES

1. Complete the acrossword puzzle to find, in the third column, a valuable asset for anyone who does puzzles.

hard stone	F	L	I	N	t
children's play	P	A	N	t	O
don't drop				t	
express exertion	g	r	u	n	t
culpability	g	u	i	l	t
type of lily		o	T		
monk	t	h	i	a	n
solid shape			O	c	
good with tools	h	a	n	d	y

2. Which point, A, B, C, or D, will balance this beam?

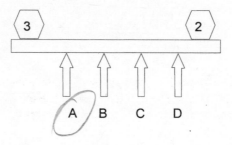

3. What word that starts with a *t* and ends with an *m* means the opposite of *keep* or *preserve*?

4. You have locked your car keys in the car, and you do not have another set of keys. All the car doors, and the luggage compartment are locked. Nevertheless, you gain entrance to the car without forcing an entry. How did you manage that?

5. Discover the hidden quotation, and the author's name.

-	E	K	R	A	L	C	C	R	U	H	T	R	A	-
E	L	B	I	S	S	O	P	M	I	E	H	T	O	T
N	I	M	E	H	T	D	N	O	Y	E	B	O	G	O
T	S	I	E	L	B	I	S	S	O	P	E	H	T	F
O	S	T	I	M	I	L	E	H	T	R	E	V	O	C
S	I	D	O	T	Y	A	W	Y	L	N	O	E	H	T

6. Thousands of years before the birth of modern crime detection methods, Sherlock Bones was called in to a village to uncover the person who ate a sacred offering to the gods. He gave every person in the village a stick of the same length, and told them to bring the sticks back to him the next morning, whereupon he would identify the thief by the fact that the thief's stick would have lengthened by two fingers. His story was an invention, but nevertheless he was able to identify the thief the next morning. How did he do that?

7. When is the next time that all three hands on this clock will appear to meet, to the nearest second?

8. Emilio has erected four wire fences in his garden, using posts a metre apart. The first, close to a tree, has 10 posts. The second, next to a hedge, has 5 posts. The third, a perimeter fence, has 11 posts, and the fourth, part of a rabbit-run, has 8 posts. How long is the total run of fencing erected by Emilio?

9. Find the American film actor/director by solving the anagram below. Two words (5, 8). Do you feel lucky? The anagram itself is not a clue.

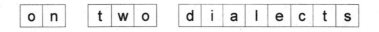

o	n		t	w	o		d	i	a	l	e	c	t	s

10. Find 15 words of at least 5 letters derived from the word *perception*. Example: centre, toner, erotic.

peptic   pincer

COPPER   prince

TIPPER

precept

price

ponce

preen

ripen

nicer

Turn to page 44 for scoring information on the creative tests.

This concludes IQ Test 4. Turn to page 122 for answers and marking details, then turn to page 109, where you will find details of how to convert your scores to an IQ rating.

Scoring

●●●●●●●●●●●●●●●●●●●●●●●●●●●●●●●●●●●●

You will gain a rough estimate of your overall IQ by completing any one of the five-part IQ tests, but you will gain a far more accurate estimate of your IQ by completing *all* of the tests.

An advantage of the way the tests in this book have been separated into discrete areas is that you can use the accumulated information from the individual tests to determine your IQ for each intelligence domain of visual-spatial, verbal-linguistic, numerical skills, logical reasoning and creative ability. Thus you can determine your strengths and weaknesses. It is only when we know what our strengths are that we can use them to their best advantage. Similarly, it is only when we face our weaknesses squarely that we can overcome them.

Understanding how you perform in each IQ domain can also be an important career pointer. If you have great numerical strengths, perhaps you should consider a career that uses those skills. You may find that you are working in entirely the wrong area. If you are a warehouse manager with very poor logical-reasoning or visual-spatial skills, you are unlikely to forge a very successful career. Focus and build on your strengths instead. If you have great linguistic or creative strengths, perhaps you should consider writing a book, or becoming an artist. (For more information concerning IQ levels and chosen careers, re-read the *Introduction*.)

If you have identified any particularly weak areas in the spectrum of your IQ, you will be able to work on eliminating those weaknesses, and this will bring up your overall IQ score. The methods of achieving this are covered in the book, *How to Boost Your IQ*, (details on page 128).

If you do not require to determine your individual scores for each IQ domain, simply average your *grand total* scores for each complete IQ test, and determine your percentage score, then read your IQ score off the graph on page 110.

To find your average score: Divide your total score for each IQ domain by 4, or by the number of tests you have completed.

(average = total ÷ number of tests completed)

To find your percentage score: Divide your achieved average score for each IQ domain, or for the tests you have completed by the maximum possible points for that test, and multiply the result by 100.

(percentage = (average ÷ maximum possible score) x 100)

Finding your IQ

1. Read along the score line until you reach the mark you achieved.
2. Draw a line up to meet the diagonal line on the graph.
3. Draw a line along to determine your IQ.

Overall IQ score, including the creativity factor

You can now determine your overall IQ by adding all five of the above IQ scores, and dividing the total by five.

Overall conventional IQ score, excluding the creativity factor

To determine your conventional IQ score, ignore the fifth test in each set and add all four other IQ scores, and divide the total by four.

Alternative method of determining overall IQ score

1. Add together your grand totals for each of the four IQ tests to get A.
2. Divide A by 1071 to get B, with creativity, or by 708 to get B without creativity.
3. Multiply B by 100 and read your score off the graph below.

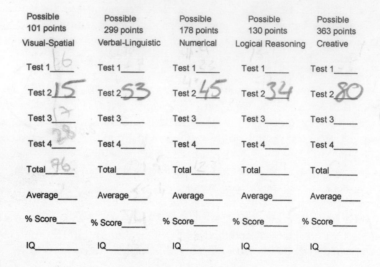

Possible 101 points Visual-Spatial	Possible 299 points Verbal-Linguistic	Possible 178 points Numerical	Possible 130 points Logical Reasoning	Possible 363 points Creative	
Test 1 _6_	Test 1 ____	Test 1 ____	Test 1 ____	Test 1 ____	
Test 2 _15_	Test 2 _53_	Test 2 _45_	Test 2 _34_	Test 2 _80_	_77·5%_
Test 3 _7_	Test 3 ____	Test 3 ____	Test 3 ____	Test 3 ____	
Test 4 _28_	Test 4 ____	Test 4 ____	Test 4 ____	Test 4 ____	
Total _96_	Total ____	Total ____	Total ____	Total ____	
Average ____	Average ____	Average ____	Average ____	Average ____	
% Score ____	% Score ____	% Score ____	% Score ____	% Score ____	
IQ ____	IQ ____	IQ ____	IQ ____	IQ ____	

Beyond the limits

The IQ tests in this book most accurately measure IQ levels of between 100 and 150. Above and below these levels IQ becomes more difficult to determine with any degree of certainty. If you managed to complete the tests in this book with great accuracy, scoring over 130 IQ points, taking less than the time permitted in most tests, it is fair to say that your IQ is probably higher than the measured level in some areas.

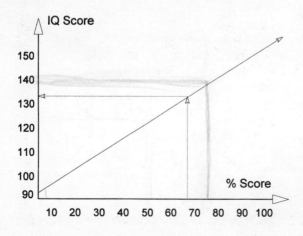

In the example shown, a percentage score of around 67 gives an IQ score of around 133 (+ or – 10%).

If your overall IQ works out to be over 130 on the scale above, which is roughly comparable with the *Cattell* scale, it could be worth having a try for Mensa membership. Details of how to get into Mensa can be found on page 126.

Answers

●●●●●●●●●●●●●●●●●●●●●●●●●●●●●●●

Test 1 <u>Part I (Visual)</u> Page 20

(2 points each problem or part, unless otherwise stated. Possible 30 total)

1. (1 point each) A & C, B & E.

2. (6 points)

3. 27 bricks (see below).

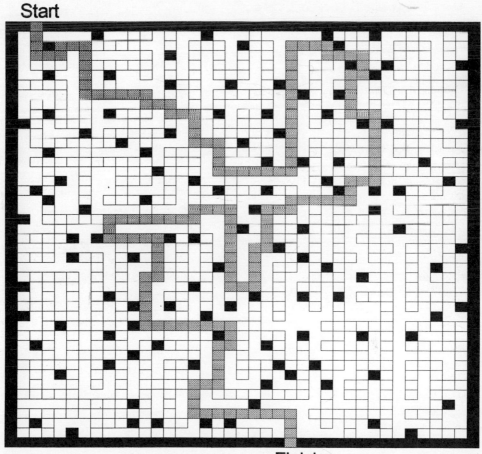

4. B.

5. B (the others are all rotated versions of the same figure).

Start

Finish

6. B (the others all spiral clockwise).

7. C (circles are analogous to hexagons).

8. C (the others are all rotated versions of the same figure).

9. C (the tiles use a top-line pattern of 231, 312, 123, 132, 321, leaving the only unused pattern, 213, which is C).

10. a. D, b. B, c. A, d. A, e. C.

Score for Part I – _____

Test 1, Part II (Words) page 25
(1 point each problem or part, unless otherwise stated. Possible 73 total)

1. (Half a point each word)

```
T M A O C Z E L T Q Q B I W
F Q K I W I F R U I T R L S
U W Q I G M F Q S W X B S W
T D C H X R M V B G U Y Q V
C I U Y M V A F I W Q D R Q
H E M F V M C R A S E G E Q
E A N A N A B N E C Z F Y P
R M W N A M O R A N G E H L
R Z Q M P G U S N X P E A R
Y E P X P V F O T C L A J B
D E J M L F L R Z V G Q H S
J F U Z E E F I G S O I X K
D L T H M Q R S Y E X S C O
```

2. a. bliss.
   b. the mother of invention.
   c. first served.
   d. the eye of the beholder.
   e. the better part of valour.

3. a. care.
   b. certainly.
   c. extraordinary.
   d. suggestibility.
   e. tiring.

4. (1 point) a and c.

5. a. paddling of ducks.
   b. leap of leopards.
   c. skulk of foxes.
   d. exhaltation of larks.
   e. clamour of rooks.

6. a. rigid, flexible.
   b. flippant, earnest.
   c. agitate, calm.
   d. flawed, perfect.
   e. insult, respect.
   f. biased, fair.
   g. erroneous, true.
   h. dwindle prosper.
   i. affect, quell.
   j. exactly, roughly.

7. a. sal.
   b. amp.
   c. mine.
   d. tin.
   e. ac.t
   f. ect.
   g. rupt.
   h. ade.
   i. ins.
   j. ris.

8. a. accumulation, reservoir.
   b. deceit, artifice.
   c. astonish, amaze.
   d. abstain, fast.
   e. goodbye, valediction.
   f. idol, effigy.
   g. calmness, equanimity.
   h. excel, surpass.
   i. repugnant, loathsome.
   j. resent, begrudge.
   k. co-ordinated, synchronised.
   l. esoteric, abstruse.
   m. enlarge, dilate.
   n. independence, autonomy.
   o. pace, celerity.
   p. permeate, pervade.
   q. sectarian, parochial.
   r. conjecture, hypothesis.

s. protagonist, enemy.

9. a. hu, b. pli, c. ab, d. bea, e. pr, f. lo, g. la, h. the, i. squ, j. wai.

10. (2 points) verbs (all others can be made from the word confusion).

Score for Part II – _____

Test 1, Part III (Numbers) page 28
(1 point each problem or part, unless otherwise stated. Possible 35 total)

1. A. 3, B. 6, C. 0, D. 4 (multiply the diagonally opposite numbers by the numbers in the middle).

2. 16. (the series reduces by 16, 8, 4, and 2).

3. 6 credits (since bananas cost 3 credits each, subtract that from 21 to get 18, then divide by 3).

4. A. 2 (multiply or divide numbers by 2 to get the numbers directly opposite).
   B. 9 (add or subtract 9 to get the numbers directly opposite).

5. A. 11 (4 x 7).   B. 32 (16 x 2).
C. 6 (9 – 3).   D. 49 (25 x 2) – 1.
E. 159 (79 x 2) + 1.   F. 146 (74 – 1) x 2.
G. 0 (5 – 5).   H. 121 (3 x 40) + 1.
I. 108 (9 x 12).

6. 2 black balls on the right and 1 white ball on the left (to make a value of 22 on each side).

7. 15 kilometres (12 + 4) – 6 (+ 5).

8. (5 points) There is only one possible route.

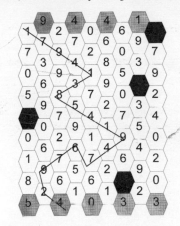

9. (5 points) E (the numbers in the missing tile must be the only combination that has not yet been used in the two previous rows on each line).

10. a. 8 (64).
b. 1 (20 ÷ 20).   c. 64 (4 x 16).
d. 50 (7 x 7) + 1.   e. 58 (5 x 12) – 2.
f. a (2nd - 1 place in alphabet).

Score for Part III – _____

Test 1, Part IV (Logic) page 32
(1 point each problem or part, unless otherwise stated. Possible 30 total)

1. False.

2. (4 points. Deduct 1 point for each wrong answer.)
Only (g) can be said for certain.

3. (5 points) 17 (circles = 4, diamonds = 5, squares = 3).

4. e (should be 'tasting : flavour').

5. a. daughter.
   b. garden.
   c. shoot.
   d. below.
   e. active.

6. B.

7. False.

8. (1 point) 1 orange, 2 green, 3 yellow, 4 blue, 5 red.

9. 10 (a = 1 + i = 9 as vowel values according to their places in the alphabet).

10. a. F, b. T, c. P, d. F, e. T, f. P, g. T, h. T, i. P, j. P.

Score for Part IV – _____

Test 1, Part V (Creativity) page 35
(1 point each problem or part, unless otherwise stated. Possible 101 total)

1. (20 points maximum. 1 point for each creative idea) Look for non-standard ideas like, _use it to file down your teeth; to smash hated music records; to heat and use as a bed-warmer; to exhibit as modern art; as a counter-weight on a see-saw for a small dog; to balance on your head while shopping so that people will talk to you; as a tombstone for a hamster; to contemplate during meditation_ …. and so on.

2. 39 blocks (to make a cube of 3 x 3 x 3 = 27).

3. (2 points) Winston Spencer Churchill.

4. (20 points maximum. One point for 5-letter words or more. Half a point for 4-letter words. Round up total to the nearest whole point.) You could have used these, or other valid words: carve, cater, cave, attic, attire, care, cite, city, crate, irate, ratty, react, rice, tacit, tact, tart, tear, trace, tract, tray, treaty, trivia, variety, veracity, very, vicar, vice, acre.

5. (2 points) There are 6 possible pairs.

6. (1 point) Tie the key to the rope that has room to swing and make it swing. Then hold onto the other rope with one hand and catch the swinging rope with the other.

7. No, you would need an extra block of 3 to make a perfect cube.

8. (18 points maximum. 1 point for each original and creative drawing.) There is no _correct_ drawing for this. Valued judgement has to be used. See pp 36 & 41-2 for more details.

9. (10 points maximum. 1 point deducted for each pause or slip-up.) This problem gets both halves of your brain fighting against each other.

10. (26 points maximum. 1 point for each that you marked _true_. No points for _false_ or _uncertain_.) If you marked more than 6 as uncertain, you need to gain more self-knowledge. If you marked more than 12 as true, you are almost certainly highly creative.

Score for Part V – _____

Grand total for Test 1 – _____

Test 2 Part I (Visual) (page 44)

(1 point each problem or part, unless otherwise stated. Possible 17 total)

1. A & E.

2. D.

3. D.

4. G (the second row of shapes should be a mirror reversal of the first row).

5. B (the same as the tall shape on its side).

6. a. C (mirror image).
   b. D (mirror image).
   c. A (mirror image).
   d. D (right white square is in the wrong place).
   e. B (mirror image).

7. C (same as first part of analogy, but standing on corner).

8. (2 points) 29 bricks (see below).

1	2	3	4	5
6	7	8	9	
10	11	12	13	14
15	16	17	18	
19	20	21	22	23
24	25	26	27	
28	29			

9. C (the others spiral clockwise).

10. (3 points) You should have been able to collect 21 diamonds.

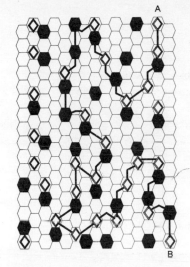

Score for Part I – _____

Test 2, Part II (Verbal) page 48
(1 point each problem or part, unless otherwise stated. Possible 77 total)

1. (3 points) e. (lettuce). The others were: a. halibut, b. flounder, c. herring, d. blowfish and f. shark.

2. (1 point per word – maximum = 13)
   a. The <u>reason</u> why rivers and seas <u>receive</u> the homage of a hundred mountain <u>streams</u> is that they keep <u>below</u> them.
   b. Every little <u>girl</u> knows about <u>love</u>. It is only her <u>capacity</u> to <u>suffer</u> for it that increases.
   c. We have genuflected before the <u>god</u> of <u>science</u> only to find that it has given us the <u>atomic</u> bomb, producing fears and <u>anxieties</u> that science can never <u>mitigate</u>.

3. a. modicum, b. cry, c. exist, d. toe, e. carpenter.

4. a. female, b. canine, c. noise, d. transport, e. homes, f. gems, g. building material, h. food, i. money, j. sibling.

5. (2 points each. Close equivalents will do.)
   a. worthy of his hire.
   b. boys.
   c. a thousand deaths.
   d. 'twixt cup and lip.
   e. played on an old fiddle.

6. a. fort, b. vert, c. vest, d. cur, e. lion,
   f. sam, g. less, h. pel, i. dow, j. note.

7. (7 points for the route. 1 point for b.)

   a.

   b. f is the only letter that does not appear.

8. (1 point each pair)
   a. parsnip, carrot (root crops).
   b. brick, concrete (man-made).
   c. photographer, model (the others are
   hardware).
   d. crystal, silver (the others are containers).
   e. go, proceed (others mean *yes*).
   f. lick, suck (the others are done with teeth).
   g. tree, wood (the others refer specifically to cut
   wood).
   h. around, throughout (others mean *internal*).
   i. designed, organised (others mean
   disorganised).
   j. abhor, despise (the others refer to actions).

9. (2 points) groaned (the others are derived
   from the word *meditation*).

10. a. shortage, b. laughter,

c. leader, d. fortunate, e. despair
f. quarrelsome.

Score for Part II –

Test 2, Part III (Numbers) page 52
(1 point each problem or part, unless otherwise
stated. Possible 54 total)

1. (1 point. There may be other solutions.)
             2 1 8 4 0
             4 0 2 1 8

2. a. 49 (7 x 7).
   b. 1.4 (14 ÷ 10).
   c. 7 (14 ÷ 2).
   d. 20 (60 ÷ 3).
   e. 4 x 40 (160).

3. a. 29 (should divide by 3).
   b. 65 (should divide by 8).
   c. 104 (should divide by 7).
   d. 20 (should divide by 6).
   e. 72 (should divide by 13).
   f. 54 (should divide by 17).
   g. 7+i (numerical position of letter in
   alphabet, plus the number, should come to 15).
   h. f11 (should be 'f12', the numerical
   position of f in the alphabet x 2).
   i. i – 5 (numerical position of the number in
   the alphabet, minus the number, should bring
   you to 3).
   j. 258 (should be 14 x 14 = 256).

4. a. 44 (12 ÷ 3 x 11).
   b. 24 ((15 – 11) x 6).
   c. 20 (34 + 6) ÷ 2.
   d. 6 (6 x 15) – 30.
   e. 35 (35 x 2) ÷ 10.

5. a. 27 (add 4).
   b. 122 (x 3) – 1.
   c. 109 (x 2) + 3.
   d. 15 (÷ 2) + 6.
   e. 59 (22 + 37).
   f. 54 (6 x 9).

g.   1 (– 4) ÷ 2.

h.   31 (– 8).

i.   34 (+ 1, 2, 4, 8…).

6. (2 points each)

  a. 10 (triangles = 2, diamonds = 3, hexagons = 4).

  b. 8 (triangles = 3, circles = 2, squares = 3).

7. (3 points each)

a. 75 km^2 (draw a line vertically down from Yvonne's house, then at 90° across to Juan's You can then calculate the area of the enclosed square at 20 x 5 = 100 km^2. Hence half of that area, i.e.. 50, is the area of the triangle. A similar process brings the area of the other triangle to 25 km^2. 25 + 50 = 75).

  b. 60 kmh (speed = distance ÷ time)

  c. Juan (to get there first, Scott would have to travel more than twice as fast as Juan).

8. (3 points) a. 2, b. 4.

Solve as simultaneous equations:

(i) 2 peaches + 4 avocados = 16,

(ii) 2 peaches + 1 avocado = 10.

Subtracting (ii) from (i), 3 avocados cost 6 credits, therefore 1 costs 2 credits. Reverting to (ii), 2 peaches cost 8 credits, so 1 peach costs 4 credits.

9. (3 points) a. 27, b. 24 (multiply by the number directly opposite, to get the number in the middle).

10. a. 9, b. 5, c. 3, d. 18, e. 29.

Score for Part III – _____

       –5

$$\frac{45}{54}$$

Test 2, Part IV (Logic) page 56

(1 point each problem or part, unless otherwise stated. Possible 45 total)

1. (2 points total)

a. – lion,

b. – tiger,

c. – spotty dog,

d. – statue of liberty,

e. – totem-pole.

2. True.

3. a. 10 (vowels).

  b. 26 (last consonant).

  c. 1 (value of vowel).

  d. 12 (first consonant + both vowels).

  e. 40 (all letters).

4. (2 points) "The only way to fail is to give up." (Read along from each letter A, B, or C, then down from the number position, to find each letter of the sentence.)

5. 7 of diamonds (all the light (red) cards should be even and the black cards odd).

6. a. F, b. T, c. F, d. F, e. F.

7. a. Z below 52, N below 28 (half numerical alphabetical position).

  b. F for Five (sequence is one, two, three, four, five).

  c. S (sequence is Thursday, Friday, Saturday, Sunday).

  d. 12 (December is the 12th month).

  e. 64 (sum value of letters in alphabetical position).

8. a. F (Mary has most),   b. P,

c. F (equal number of yellow),   d. T,   e. T,

f. T,   g. P,   h. F (they have 12),   i. P.

9. (5 points) Follow the moves as shown.

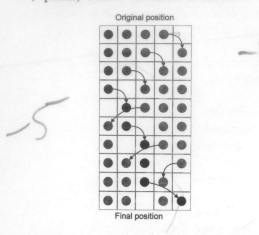

Original position

Final position

10. b. C, c. AC, d. AC, e. AC, f. C, g. AC, h. C, i. C, j. AC.

Score for Part IV – _____

Test 2, Part V (Creativity) page 60
(1 point each problem or part, unless otherwise stated. Possible 100 total)

1. (5 points) The planks are cut as shown and wedged into the walls to provide a strong temporary bridge. There may be other valid solutions. See below

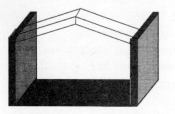

2. (40 points maximum. 2 point for each valid word) Here are 25 you could have used: cache, cash, mash, hash, bash, flash, trash, smash, rash, sash, slash, thrash, lash, balderdash, calabash, gnash, dash, abash, moustache, stash, gash, splash, brash, clash, eyelash.

3. (3 points) You fell through the ceiling.

4. (1 point for each highly creative solution. 16 points maximum. No points for *climbing the stairs*, or *going up a ladder*. See Test 1, Part V for more details on the type of thinking required.)

5. (5 points) The most logical solution is to hit the banana with the plank to make it swing, then quickly put the plank against a wall and climb it and catch the swinging banana, but perhaps you came up with a more creative one, such as, 'knock a hole in the ceiling with the plank, then lean the plank against a wall, climb up to the top of the plank and out through the hole, then kick another hole in the ceiling near the banana and hoist it up.'

6. (2 points) You haven't hit the ground yet.

7. (2 points) c. Neither. There is an equal quantity of milk in the water and water in the milk.

8. (2 points) It is downhill all the way.

9. (5 points) The shadow of the tree will be proportional to the length of the tree as the stick is proportional to the length of its own shadow. If, for example, the stick's height is 5 units long, and it's shadow is 6 units long, then the tree's height will be the length of its shadow times 5, divided by 6, or five-sixths the length of its shadow.

10. (20 points maximum) 1 point for each suggestion if they are of a similar or better quality than – *lower it into a volcano by helicopter until it reaches the temperature of boiling water,* or *stick it back up a chicken's bottom, and boil the chicken.*

Score for Part V – _____ 85/100

Grand total for Test 2 – _____

Test 3 Part I (Visual) page 64

(1 point each problem or part, unless otherwise stated. Possible 20 total)

1. a. D, b. C, c. D, d. C, e. A.

2. F (the shape on its left side).

3. G (in the bottom row, black shapes become white, and vice-versa, but shaded shapes remain the same).

4. G (the missing shape on its left side).

5. E (the lower diamond should be dark).

6. C.

7. D (the sequence for both the petals and the sides of the surrounding shape is 3, 4, 5, 6).

8. a. D, b. C, c. D, d. B, e. A (most are mirror-images, but in 'e', the right-hand white ball should be in the upper left of the square instead of the lower left).

9. (2 points) "Dost thou love life? Then do not squander time, for that is the stuff life is made of."   *Benjamin Franklin*

10. (2 points) E (the above tile, on its right side, with the only animal not yet used in this row).

Score for Part I –

Test 3 Part II (Verbal) page 69
(1 point each problem or part, unless otherwise stated. Possible 87 total)

1. a. et, b. ald, c. act, d. chic, e. lar,
f. vine, g. gal, h. pse, i. el, j. cle.

2. a. never boils.
   b. gathers no moss.
   c. is a penny gained.
   d. lead to Rome.
   e. tell no tales.

3. a. inept, b. verbose, c. extrude,
d. temperate, e. evaluate.

4. a. kestrel, b. parrot,
    c. dolphin, d. tarantula,
    e. tortoise, f. armadillo,
    g. peacock, h. albatross,
    i. crocodile, j. caterpillar.

5. a. juncture, b. falter,
    c. compress, d. stalwart,
    e. august, f. sluggish,
    g. jeopardy, h. terminal,
    i. blissful, j. nucleus.

6. a. inapt, inappropriate.
    b. burden, handicap.
    c. docile, submissive.
    d. error, fallacy.
    e. chaste, pure.
    f. release, extricate.

7. a. gra, b. str, c. cla, d. cha, e. be, f. ab,
g. tea, h. pur, i. wre, j. fo.

8. (Half a point each)
a. hearing, b. native,
c. unimportant, d. compassion,
e. different, f. refined, g. droll,
h. steady, i. unequivocal,
j. treachery.

9. (1 point each word – maximum = 18.)
   a. There are few things impossible in themselves; it is the application to achieve them that we lack more than the means.
   b. With our actions, we communicate our most deeply held values and beliefs, and through the global influence of our mass media, even the simplest actions we take have the power to influence and move people of all nations.

c. Most of us have no adequate <u>conception</u> of our inherent powers and <u>abilities</u>. At heart, we <u>underestimate</u> ourselves. We do not really <u>believe</u> in ourselves and for that reason remain weak, <u>ineffectual</u>, even impotent, when we could be strong, <u>dominant</u>, victorious.

d. It is the <u>prerogative</u> of genius to confer a measure of itself upon inferior intelligences. In reading the works of Milton, Bacon, and Newton, <u>thoughts</u> greater than the growth of our own minds are transplanted into them; and feelings more profound, <u>sublime</u>, or comprehensive are <u>insinuated</u> amidst our ordinary train.

10. (maximum 8 points. 1 point for each cowboy word up to 6. 2 points for finding the item of underwear – *brassiere*.)

```
B L G S K A G I R G I G O K I G O
E E O J F I G K A O K A L A U K U
A F D B A J A S G I G E G R S R A
K O G R S O G U E R N G S G U G S
S G G A Q U G J G E E L D D A S U
A I I S A L A E A T U V A R U B I
F A G S U O L A S S O I Q O U N O
E U G I R H G R U L I G U K A G S
I M U E E R U G K O G K L I V O I
H K A R I F L E A H A W U R I E U
C U R E U G U G U U K U I G U U R
R I A I O U G A S E Q A U K E S
E G O K O K E T P U G U R G R G U
K U G U G U E A A O A K I S U G U
C A I E A T O U H A U S P U E A N
E K G U S U R G C U E U U R A U S
N U I Q U I K U U R R U G G U G U
U A N U I G O I O S A E A I O K A
```

<u>Score for Part II</u> – 48

<u>Test 3 Part III (Numerical)</u> page 73
(1 point each problem or part, unless otherwise stated. Possible 37 total)

1. a. 28 (multiply opposite numbers to get the middle ones).
   b. 15 (add opposite numbers to get the numbers in the middle).

2. (2 points each) a. 6, b. 13 (see answer to Test 2, Part III, question 8, for detailed instructions on how to solve this type of problem).

3. 24 (the total of the numbers in the small hexagons).

4. a. 42 (6 x 7)
   b. 56 (8 x 7)
   c. 36 (12 x 3)
   d. 105 ((x 2) – 1)
   e. 3 (add the components of each number to get the next. Since 3 is the only component in the last numbered box, the solution is 3)
   f. 77 (65 + 12)
   g. l (i + 3 alphabetical places)
   h. j + q (alphabetical places add to 27, with the first letter rising 2, 3 and 4 places, and the last letter going down by 2, 3 and 4 places)
   i. 26 (alphabetical places add to 26)
   j. 2 (alphabetical places of last letter of jab.)

5. (2 points) 8 (the black balls are worth 7, so 2 black balls = 14. 70 – 14 = 56; 56 ÷ 7 = 8).

6. a. 16 (black = 4, grey = 1, white = 4).
   b. 10 (black = 4, grey = 4, white = 1).
   c. 8 (black = 3, grey = 10, white = 1).
   d. 11 (black = 2, grey = 3, white = 3).
   e. 20 (black = 3, grey = 2, white = 7).

7. a. 14, b. 28, c. 39, d. 9, e. 21.

8. a. 11 (diamonds = 4, circles = 3, triangles = 5).
   b. 12 (circles = 4, triangles = 3, squares = 5).

9. (2 points each) a. 5km (when Sandy has passed Dee's house by 5 km).
   b. 55 minutes. (10 minutes for the first leg, and 45 for the second. Use the formula, speed = distance ÷ time).

10. (2 points) This is the only possible route.

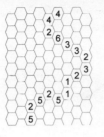

<u>Score for Part III</u> – 24

<u>Test 3 Part IV (Logic)</u> page 78
(1 point each problem or part, unless otherwise
stated. Possible 25 total)

1. (3 points) 23 (bricks = 3, cups = 7, rugs = 2).

2. (2 points) c and h.

3. c (if you know that a person is never truthful,
then true means false, and vice-versa).

4. (5 points. Read down and along to get each
letter.) "If you would win a man to your cause,
first convince him that you are his sincere
friend."
                            – Abraham Lincoln

5. a. F, b. T, c. F, d. F, e. T.

6. C (diamond is missing).

7. Pour out the liquid until it just touches the
bottom rim of the beaker. At this point it will be
half-full.

8. 8 hours (a hole twice as long, wide and deep
will be 8 times the volume).

9. (3 points for all correct)
a. Sandy, b. John, c. Gail, d. Lorraine, e.
Nicola, f. Colin, g. Lorna, h. Fraser.

10. (3 points) Butterfly.

<u>Score for Part IV</u> – 17.

<u>Test 3 Part V (Creativity)</u> page 81
(1 point each problem or part, unless otherwise
stated. Possible 101 total)

1. a. 53.
   b. 255 (making a block of 11 x 4 x 7).
   c. 211 (by removing the top block, making a
block of 11 x 4 x 6).

2. (20 points maximum. 1 point each word)
Here are 25 you could have used: plain, plane,
slain, train, terrain, crane, drain, domain,
grain, retain, explain, retain, ordain, chain,
strain, urbane, inane, disdain, profane,
ascertain, abstain, restrain, migrain, complain,
cellophane.

3. (20 points maximum. 1 point for ideas such as:
*a mould for balloons; eyes on a snowman; a
pestle for crushing cornflakes; a fishing float; a
floating ornament for a garden pond, a per-
cussion instrument; no points for ideas such as to
light a room.* See Test 1, Part V for more details).

4. (18 points maximum) See Test 1, Part V for
details of how to judge the drawings.

5. (4 points) 6 (the roller moves along half a
metre for every metre that the flask moves, thus
reducing the number of turns required).

6.

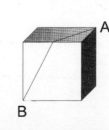

7.

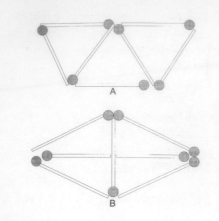

8. B (the only one which does not have a liquid content).

9. (1 point each valid word of at least 4 letters. 2 points for words of more than four letters, up to a maximum of 20 points.) You could have used: animating, nation, ingot, moaning, among, maintain, again, among, mint, minting, tang, mango, taming, anoint, giant, gain, atom, ingot, moat, minion, naming, amino, manna, mania, atoning.

10. (12 points maximum) The word is *inspiration*.

imagines	t	h	i	n	k	s
crave or long for	h	a	n	k	e	r
lucky symbol	m	a	s	c	o	t
small towel or bib	n	a	p	k	i	n
tests	t	r	i	a	l	s
marching display	p	a	r	a	d	e
gratitude	t	h	a	n	k	s
ringed planet	s	a	t	u	r	n
plague or pestilence	b	l	i	g	h	t
saggy	d	r	o	o	p	y
seeker	h	u	n	t	e	r

Score for Part V – 40

Grand total for Test 3 –

Test 4 Part I (Visual) page 88
(1 point each problem or part, unless otherwise stated. Possible 34 total)

1. L.

2. G.

3. C.

4. a. D.
   b. B.
   c. B.
   d. D.
   e. A.

5. a. A & C, b. B & E, c. B & C, d. B & D, e. C & D.

6. (3 points) 4 blocks. The further along the scale, the greater the proportional weight effect of each block. To balance another block at position 8 requires 4 blocks at position 2. 4 x 2 = 1 x 8.

7. C (object stands on its left side, and the outer and inner shapes swap colours).

8. (1½ points per answer

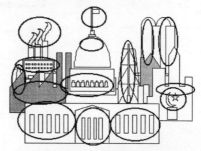

9. B (the others all have alternating background and foreground colours).

10. D.

Score for Part I –

Test 4, Part II (Verbal)4 page 94
(1 point each problem or part, unless otherwise stated. Possible 62 total)

1. a. hollow, b. mingle, c. invade, d. perfect,
e. hang, f. blockade, g. cadaver, h. brag, i.
curator, j. squall.

2. a. saves nine.
   b. than the devil you don't.
   c. to find a thief.
   d. the one-eyed man is king.
   e. fell great oaks.

3. a. liturgy, b. spiritual, c. sniff,
d. sacrosanct, e. ephemeral.

4. a. conjecture, b. sanction,
c. acquiesce.

5. (7 points) The cat is a *leopard*.

```
P Y U Z V U F E C U E U C J Q Y
A I W C E A Z N S F B K C F Z F
R L Z T W A G F D R K G W X A N
R O E J S O P A A U K A V G Q M
O B L R P X Z L H L C W D B E O
T G V R T Y P C M A O X G L J X
J P E E L S V O M J A L G C X I
X R I C G M E N Y K E A U Z B M
O X I X S X B K A O E R Q I N E
G S H G G W N I P X L S S R A X
D N F D E V J A D E D C Z X W H
V S P U I O R H W Y R R B D N Z
L W O N D D N S F N E O V J V D
K R H X S Z X X S G F W O C K G
I M K I N G F I S H E R F E V F
O U E S P A R R O W Z D S Q A Z
```

6. a. organised, random.
   b. nebulous, clear.
   c. base, noble.
   d. rapport, conflict.
   e. concomitant, attending.

7. a. microlight, b. gyroplane, c. glider,
   d. helicopter, e. seaplane, f. spaceship,
   g. divebomber, h. airship, i. rocket,
   j. aeroplane.

8. a. flesh, meat.
   b. intimate, insinuate.
   c. invalidate, abrogate.
   d. inconstant, fickle.
   e. abate, wane.

9. a. lea, b. br, c. alle, d. wri, e. res, f. bu.

10. (1 point each word)

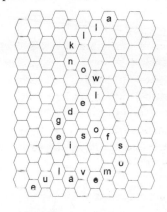

Score for Part II

Test 4, Part III (Numerical) page 98
(1 point each problem or part, unless otherwise stated. Possible 52 total)

1. a. 6 (6 x 1).
    b. 48 (12 x 4), next would be 16 (12 + 4).
    c. 30 (23 + 7).
    d. 62 (49 + 13).
    e. 3.75 (9.5 – 2) ÷ 2.
    f. 141 (x 2) + 2.
    g. 114 (58 – 1) x 2.
    h. 45 (18 – 3) x 3.
    i. 75 (60 + 15).
    j. 28bh (14 + 14 = 28; b is 2nd letter, h is 8th letter).

2. (5 points for all correct. Solution is in the black squares)

7	2	9	1	6
1	6	7	2	9
2	9	1	6	7
6	7	2	9	1
9	1	6	7	2

3. a. 8, b. 5, c. 3, d. 12, e. 9.

4. a. 15 credits per barrel (the change does not affect the cost).
  b. 2 credits per wooget.

5. (4 points) 3 (add the three top numbers together, and subtract the total from the result of the three bottom numbers added together).

6. a. 9 (grey = 1, black = 2, white = 3).
  b. 16 (grey = 3, black = 5, white = 1).
  c. 12 (grey = 4, black = 3, white = 1).
  d. 11 (grey = 1, black = 3, white = 4).
  e. 17 (grey = 5, black = 2, white = 3).

7. a. 6, b. 4.

8. (3 points each)
a. 8 (crosses = 3, hexagons = 4, triangles = 2).
b. 16 (crosses = 6, circles = 3, squares = 4).

9. a. Saturday, b. Monday, c. Thursday, d. Sunday, e. 2.

10. (2 points for a, 3 points for b, 3 for c.)
  a. 337.5 units^3 (length x breadth x height of all the boxes added together).
  b. 216 (length x breadth of each of the 6 surfaces, added together).
  c. 8 (22.5, the volume of the smallest box, goes into 180, 8 times).

Score for Part III –

Test 4 Part IV (Logic) page 102
(1 point each problem or part, unless otherwise stated. Possible 30 total)

1. (3 points) 4 (no map needs more than 4 colours to differentiate the boundaries).

2. a. F, b. T, c. F.

3. (3 points) C.

4. a. bloom, b. climb, c. previously, d. dreamy, e. tease.

5. (1 point) A & D and B & C.

6. (1 point) 1 yellow, 2 blue, 3 red, 4 green, 5 orange.

7. a. F (five), b. M (May), c. W (Wednesday).

8. a. False (John may not be in the playground).
    b. False (Anthea may have run, but not finished).
    c. True.

9. a. essential, b. non-essential c. essential, d. non-essential, e. essential.

10. a. AC.
    b. AC.
    c. G (which is why we switch to a smaller gear when travelling uphill on a bicycle).

Score for Part IV –

Test 4 Part V (Creativity) 8
page 106
(1 point each problem or part, unless otherwise
stated. Possible 61 total)

1. (10 points max. 1 point per word.)
The word in the shaded column is *intuition*.

hard stone	f	l	i	n	t
children's play	p	a	n	t	o
don't drop	c	a	t	c	h
express exertion	g	r	u	n	t
culpability	g	u	i	l	t
type of lily	l	o	t	u	s
monk, like Tuck	f	r	i	a	r
solid shape	b	l	o	c	k
good with tools	h	a	n	d	y

2. B.

3. (3 points) Transform.

4. A window was open.

5. (4 points. The quote is written backwards,
starting from the bottom right)
"The only way to discover the limits of the
possible is to go beyond them into the
impossible." – Arthur C. Clarke

6. (3 points) The guilty person cut two fingers'
length from his stick before taking it to
Sherlock Bones.

7. (3 points) To the nearest second the hands
will appear to meet at 3.16, and 16 seconds. In
reality the hands do not meet exactly until
midnight and midday. As the minute hand turns,
the hour hand also turns.

8. (3 points) 30 metres (count the spaces, not
the posts).

9. (3 points) Clint Eastwood .

10. (1 point for 5 letter words, 2 points for
longer words up to 30 points.)
You could have used these, or any other valid
words: *reception, precept, entire, notice,
pioneer, copier, creep, poetic, cretin, protein,
repent, tropic, piece, nicer, recent, receipt,
tenor, topic, percent, copper, enter.*

Score for Part V – _____

Grand total for Test 4 – _____

Grand totals carried forward

Test 1   Test 2

Test 3   Test 4

How to get into Mensa
● ●

How to get into Mensa

If your intelligence lies in the top two per cent of the population, there is a good chance that you feel somewhat isolated. Very few of the people you talk to are able to converse with you on the same level. That is one of the reasons Mensa, an international organisation dedicated to identifying and fostering human intelligence for the benefit of humanity, was formed. Mensa provides a forum for intellectual exchange among members, with various mutually beneficial activities, including lectures by the greatest thinkers of our day, a monthly magazine delivered to your home each month, special interest groups, social activities, and hospitality for travellers. (There are Mensans all over the world who allow other members to stay with them free of charge.)

The only way into Mensa is through a strictly administered IQ test in which you must score in the top two percent of the population. There are no other restrictions. Mensa is discrimination free. Qualifications, age, gender, race, creed, colour, appearance, location, and physical ability don't matter. The only thing that matters is passing the test. The procedure is uncomplicated. Mensa supply a standard home test which you take as a preliminary eliminator. It takes an hour to complete. If you score high enough in that test you are invited to take a supervised test at your nearest Mensa test centre. There is one in every major city in the UK. That test takes about 2 hours in total, and includes a 'culture-fair' section which consists mainly of visual-spatial type questions. This is not marked unless you fail the main *Cattell* type test, which consists of a mixture of verbal-linguistic, logical, numeric, and visual-spatial questions. You will be offered the chance to take a short break between tests. Take advantage of the offer.

If you fail the Mensa test there is still hope. Many who initially fail the entrance test get in at the second attempt, after becoming more familiar with the methods of solution for IQ tests.

Mensa can be contacted at the following addresses

UK
British Mensa Ltd.
Mensa House
St John's Square
Wolverhampton
WV2 4AH

USA
American Mensa Ltd
2626 East 14th Street
Brooklyn
New York
NY11235–3992

International
Mensa International Ltd.
15 The Ivories
6 – 8 Northampton St
London N1 2HY

Australia
Australian Mensa Inc.
PO Box 213
Toorak
Victoria

Canada
Mensa Canada Society
PO Box 505
Sta
Toronto
Ontario M5M 4L8

Internet Sites for Mensa

UK:	http://www.mensa.org.uk
USA:	http://www.us.mensa.org
Canada:	http://www.rohcg.on.ca/mensa/mensa.html
Australia:	http://www.au.mensa.org/
South Africa:	http://www.mickey.laccess.za/~martin/mensa/
New Zealand:	http://kiwimall.co.nz/other/mensa.1mensa.html
Sweden:	http://www.mensa.se

* *

Further IQ testing

IQ testing is the single most accurate way of determining the success potential of job and college applicants. The one thing you can guarantee about people is that if they are intelligent today, they'll be intelligent tomorrow. When combined with a personality test, the probability of selecting the right candidate by these tests increases still further.

John Bremner is involved with ThinkWare™, a company that produces both self-marking and return-for-marking general IQ tests and job-specific aptitude tests and personality tests. Additionally, a Windows™ PC based IQ test will soon be available from ThinkWare.

If you want to select your employees on true merit rather than on the ability to conduct interviews, or on the ability to sweet-talk line managers, outline your requirements to ThinkWare by email at the following address:

think@zetnet.co.uk

IQ Bibliography and Recommended Reading

(Authors in Alphabetical order)

Test Your Own Aptitude	*Barrett & Williams*	(Kogan Page)
Bartlett's Familiar Quotations	*E.M. Beck (Editor)*	(Macmillan)
How to Boost Your IQ	*John Bremner*	(Ward-Lock)
Mensa New Number Puzzles	*John Bremner*	(Carlton Books)
The Mind Map Book	*Tony Buzan*	(BBC Books)
Quantum Learning	*Bobbi DePorter*	(Piatkus)
Know Your Own IQ	*H. J. Eysenck*	(Penguin)
Sense & Nonsense in Psychology	*H.J. Eysenck*	(Pelican)
Autobiography	*Benjamin Franklin*	(Oxford U. Press)
Nature of Human Intelligence	*J.P. Guilford*	(McGraw-Hill)
Intelligence and Personality	*A. Heim*	(Pelican)
IQ in the Meritocracy	*R. J. Herrnstein*	(Allen Lane)
Blueprints for Memory	*William D. Hersey*	(Amacom)
Unlimited Success	*Napoleon Hill*	(Piatkus)
Think and Grow Rich	*Napoleon Hill*	(Piatkus)
A. Einstein, Creator and Rebel	*B. Hoffmann*	(H-D MacGibbon)
Memory Facts and Fallacies	*I.M.L. Hunter*	(Pelican)
Educability and Group Differences	*A. R. Jensen*	(Methuen)
Maths in Context	*Modular Maths Organization*	(Heineman)
Correct Me If I'm Wrong	*Rosemary Moor*	(Stanley Thornes)
Psychology You can Use	*William H. Roberts*	(Harcourt, Brace)
Awaken the Giant Within	*Anthony Robbins*	(Simon &Schuster)
Applied Imagination	*Alex F. Osborne*	(C. Schribner's Sons)
Have a Great Day	*Norman V. Peale*	(Giniger Company)
Test Your IQ	*Pirie & Butler*	(Pan Books)
Brain Power	Savant & Fleischer	(Piatkus)
A Guide to Intelligence and Personality Testing	*V. Serbriakoff*	(Parthenon Publishing)
Maximise Your Mental Power	*David. J. Schwart*	(Thorsons)
Test Your Intelligence	*Norman Sullivan*	(Blandford/Cassell)
The Success System That Never Fails	*W. C. Stone*	(Harper Collins)
The Oxford Companion to the Mind	*Various*	(Oxford Uni. Press)
Readings in Human Intelligence	*S. Wiseman*	(University Paperbacks)